Justice for Children

Justice for Children

Allison Morris, Henri Giller,
Elizabeth Szwed and Hugh Geach

M

First published 1980 by
THE MACMILLAN PRESS LTD
London and Basingstoke
Associated companies in Delhi Dublin
Hong Kong Johannesburg Lagos Melbourne
New York Singapore and Tokyo

Printed in Great Britain by
J. W. Arrowsmith Limited
Bristol

British Library Cataloguing in Publication Data

Justice for children.
1. Juvenile delinquency – England
2. Rehabilitation of juvenile delinquents – England 3. Juvenile justice, Administration of – England
I. Morris, Allison
364.6 HV9146.A5

ISBN 0-333-27486-5
ISBN 0-333-27487-3 Pbk

Contents

Part II Care and Justice

Introduction

Children have not always been seen as a distinct social problem. Until this century, childhood was a brief and unimportant phase of life; infant mortality rates were high and those children who survived were quickly introduced into the responsibilities of adult life. As children had neither rights nor independent status, they were vulnerable to all forms of physical and economic exploitation and abuse. Intervention into family life was virtually unknown, since the principle of family autonomy was supported in many influential sections of society (both secular and religious). The history of childhood, and the history of children as a social problem, are primarily a history of changes in the legal and social relations of children with the adult world.

Children as legal subjects

Initially the concept of childhood was peripheral to law. The various legal capacities and incapacities attributed to the young only tangentially alluded to differences between children and adults as social beings; hence, in the nineteenth century, although males could marry at 14 they could not dispose of their property until they were 21. The law recognised only infancy and adulthood; the term 'infant' included both the new-born babe and the youth in his 21st year.

Changes in the legal status of children first emerged in the common-law courts and the Court of Chancery, jurisdictions which regulated legal relations, particularly property interests. The doctrine of *parens patriae* (the doctrine which legitimated state intervention between parents and children and formed a basis for the regulation of these relationships) developed from the need to control the property interests of those legally disbarred from holding land. Initially the Court of Chancery was not the guardian of *all* children: those without property were considered to be outside its jurisdiction.

During the nineteenth century, however, the doctrine of *parens patriae* encompassed a greater number of children as the judiciary became increasingly willing to interpose itself between parents (usually fathers) and their offspring. By adopting the rhetoric of promoting the 'welfare of the child', the courts expanded their jurisdiction into social as well as property relationships within the family. 'Welfare' was taken in its widest sense, the moral and religious welfare of the child being considered in addition to his physical well-being.

But the doctrine of *parens patriae* was only partially concerned with the *quality* of life provided for children. The courts' main concern was the regulation of *adults*' interests. So, for example, the concept of the 'welfare of the child' was used to curtail fathers' absolute rights to the custody of their children and to expand mothers' rights to custody. It was not used to protect the child from abuse or neglect by parents. The courts adopted an interventionist role in relation to children's particular interests only after these concerns had developed in other areas of social life. The first Prevention of Cruelty to Children Act did not come until 1879, 75 years after legislation on the prevention of cruelty to animals.

While the courts recognised the status of childhood as a legal phenomenon, the children concerned did not become legal subjects in their own right. They were merely the *objects* of intervention. It was the judiciary rather than the child that was the arbiter of what was in the 'welfare of the child'. In one reported case a young student who wished to attend Oxford University was compelled by the court to attend the University of Cambridge, as this was what his guardian wanted!

Children as social problems

These features provided the law with sufficient flexibility to control the organisation of childhood once certain kinds of socialisation were perceived as social problems. By positing the legal status of children as being dependent both on the need for *protection* and on the need for *control*, the law could place children in a juridical no man's land subject to the intervention of others (the state, parents, schools, social services, the medical profession and so on). This gradual recognition of the legal status of childhood by the courts in the nineteenth century was only one of a number of devices whereby the state could legitimately interpose in what had hitherto been the private social arrangements of the adult world. The doctrine of *parens patriae* was a vehicle through which social relations could be regulated. Throughout the nineteenth century increasing attention was paid to the development of family life as the primary mechanism of a disciplined socialisation. The young were the barometers of the efficiency of the family as an agency of socialisation. State intervention into family life through judicial proceedings provided one means by which acceptable family practices could be enforced.

The history of children as social problems is not found in the development of legal arrangements for the young propertied classes. Influential in this is the series of legal regulations which were developed to deal with the propertyless classes – in particular, the development of a distinct juvenile justice system to deal with children who broke the criminal law.

Until the middle of the nineteenth century both adults and children were subject to the same laws and penalties – imprisonment, hanging, flogging. In 1833, for example, a 9-year-old boy was sentenced to death for pushing a stick through a cracked window and pulling out some printer's colours, the value of which was two pence. The only exception to this rule was that where the child was under 14, he was presumed to be incapable of committing crimes (*doli incapax*). After the age of seven, however, this presumption was rebuttable and was usually considered rebutted by the fact of the offence.

Far from reflecting the benevolence of the judiciary, this rule was part of a wider concept central to the criminal law: the actor must possess a guilty mind (*mens rea*) for culpability to be attached to the commission of the offence (*actus reus*). Punishment was justified only in such cases. For those presumed not to understand evil (the young and the mad), punishment was inappropriate.

Concern with the growth of crime generally at the beginning of the nineteenth century, and especially 'the alarming increase in juvenile crime', created the basis of a new social problem: the rapid accumulation of the labouring classes in the cities heightened awareness of the indisciplined mob. Crime and civil disobedience were epitomised in one class – the working class – and the criminal trade in which they engaged was seen as a direct product of the degenerate social conditions within which they lived. Early investigations into the aetiology of juvenile delinquency (such as the report of the Committee into Crime in the Metropolis in 1816) identified as causes of delinquency squalid living conditions, the poor moral climate in which children were brought up and the rigorous application of harsh laws. To this the moral topographers of the time (for example, Mayhew and Chadwick) added volumes of empirical data which sought to identify the dishonest labouring classes – the 'dangerous class'. Youth was a key part of this. Chadwick, for example, cites several instances of 'great havoc' committed by 'mere boys' and comments that:

> A population that is young, inexperienced, ignorant, credulous, irritable, passionate and dangerous [has] a perpetual tendency to moral as well as physical deterioration (Poor Law Commission, 1842, p. 203).

Reducing the harsh penalties of the criminal law and improving the living conditions of the labouring poor were unpalatable remedies. But belief in the moral degeneracy of offenders and in the malleability and reformation of juvenile offenders suggested a form of intervention which was thought to be effective yet left untouched the foundations of the existing socio-political structure. Reformation by segregation was seen as the panacea for crime by the pioneers of the reformatory movement. For example, Matthew Davenport Hill, a pioneer of the reformatory movement, wrote:

> [The delinquent] is a little stunted man already – he knows much and a great deal too much of what is called life – he can take care of his own immediate interests. He is self-reliant, he has so long directed or misdirected his own actions and has so little trust in those about him, that he submits to no control and asks for no protection. He has consequently much to unlearn – he has to be turned again into a child (Hill, 1855, p. 5).

These developments were matched by changes in the legal processes for dealing with children. Attempts to reduce the stigma of full criminal process and, thereby, to reduce the child's affiliation to a life of crime were constantly rejected during the first part of the nineteenth century but, by the 1850s, summary trial for juvenile offenders who had committed minor thefts was possible. These procedures, however, remained the exception rather than the rule. It was not until 1908 that a distinct tribunal for children was established: the juvenile court. Its primary purpose was to punish the child for his conduct.

But these new juvenile courts also had responsibility over children who were suffering from cruelty and neglect (be it malicious or circumstantial). This, like the court's criminal jurisdiction, had also developed throughout the nineteenth century. It was believed that the 'dangerous class' could transmit crime, like a disease, to those living in conditions which made them susceptible to infection – the 'perishing classes'. To combat this susceptibility in the 'perishing classes', the law was extended to intervene in particular social conditions, not in themselves illegal, which were said to exacerbate delinquent development. Mary Carpenter, when presenting her case for establishing reformatory schools, claimed that by reforming children rather than punishing them the public would be less reluctant to bring children to court and the state would thereby be more able to remove them from the streets.

Hence, by 1866 magistrates could commit to industrial schools children who were vagrant, who were said by their parents to be incorrigible or who were associating with criminals and prostitutes, so that they could be resocialised or reformed. In the name of 'rescue' vast numbers of children were brought under the umbrella of the state. By 1894 over 17 000 children from the 'perishing classes' were held in industrial schools, compared with a mere 4800 delinquent children in the reformatories.

Children as an allegory

The recognition of childhood was one device by which control of the property-less class was achieved. The need for special rules, procedures and institutions for dealing with juveniles was essential once childhood was seen as a distinct social phenomenon. But the creation of childhood was only a part of deeper structural changes in British society.

At the beginning of the nineteenth century, child labour was universal and inescapable. The family was employed as a whole and worked together just as it had done in the past. The kinship system determined the training, earnings and discipline of the family; and although discipline was harsh, it was socially tolerable because it came from the child's father. There was no state protection against abuse: the child was regarded as the property of the father, and as such was 'protected' from state interference; but, more importantly, the state itself was reluctant to interfere because the child played an essential role in maintaining trade. As the century advanced, there was a growing feeling of revulsion against the working conditions of children; but the real effect on child labour did not occur until the breakdown of the kinship system, which itself resulted from technological advances. Parents and children no longer worked together – the 1833 Factories Act limited the working hours of children and, by snapping the link between the child's shift and that of the adult, broke the kinship system – and the harsh discipline once administered by the father was now exercised by the foreman. Depersonalisation prompted statutory interference.

Statutes not only restricted the working day of the child; they also took an interest in his moral upbringing. This found expression in the development of compulsory education, the expansion of Poor Law relief and the increasing number of measures which sought to protect children from parental abuse. The strategies by which these developments were put into practice (schools, workhouses, children's homes) formed part of a wide network of disciplinary control. Inherent in the process of identifying 'dangerous' and 'perishing' classes was the belief that there existed the ideal of an 'honest labouring class'. Legislation for controlling deviant youth was directed at achieving this ideal.

So, for example, the reformatories and industrial schools were continually asked to reproduce conditions which were the 'epitome of working class society'. As social conditions changed, so, too, did the schools. In the 1850s and 1860s the conditions of the working class in society legitimated the kinds of jobs which children in the reformatories were given: monotonous jobs which provided them with the habits of industrial discipline. Later on, when the social demand was for a literate work-force adept at basic technical skills, the institutions became educationally oriented.

In this way children reflect social and economic relations within society, and troublesome children (both the delinquent and the destitute) illustrate not only the content of this but also the tensions within it. Society felt compelled to do 'something'. The vital difference between these two groups, at least initially, was that intervention in the life of the delinquent was based upon his *conduct* (a matter over which he was assumed to have responsibility), whereas intervention in the life of the neglected child was based on his *status* (a matter over which he was assumed to have no responsibility). Hence, the pioneers of the reformatory movement vigorously argued for the clear separation of the delinquent (in reformatories) and the destitute (in industrial schools).

Gradually, however, this distinction became less clear. By 1896 an official committee into the working of the reformatories and industrial schools had stated that the children in the two institutions were in the main the same and that there was no substantial difference in the discipline and regime in the institutions. The expansion of the child care service in the twentieth century and the development of preventive social work both served further to consolidate children in trouble into a single conceptual category: the deprived and the depraved were one and the same. Couched in the language of 'welfare' and supported by an army of professionals, attention was continually diverted from what children *do* to what children *are*. Children became the *object* of our concern, rarely its *subject*. Consequently children became ensnared in a series of discretionary processes within which the safeguarding of the rights of individual children was subordinated to what were seen as wider social problems. This trend culminated in the Children and Young Persons Act 1969.

Children generally have become the focus of increasing professional intervention and attention. With the advance of treatment ideology in twentieth-century penal policy, and its influence on the practice of the courts in relation to children, it is not surprising that the juvenile court has become an arena in which the 'helping' professions seek to make their mark on the children who come before it.

The bulk of the children subject to juvenile court proceedings have committed delinquent acts or have been abused or neglected. The treatment approach suggests that there is little difference between the social and psychological environment of these children. The causes of both can be 'diagnosed' and 'cured' by a course of 'treatment'. But there is mounting controversy about whether involuntary treatment, prescribed by the court and social services, can be anything but punishment. Research shows that neglected as well as delinquent children feel that they are being punished and not treated by the courts. Yet, judicial impartiality and fairness, especially in dispositions, has been severely affected by notions of treatment. This has resulted, on occasions, in grave injustice to children. To make matters worse the present juvenile court system and the disposition alternatives available to it are manifestly unsuccessful: there is an increasing body of opinion which believes that 'treatment' can have a negative effect on a child and his family.

The juvenile court is also expected to fulfil two incompatible roles. It is concerned with the child's welfare but at the same time it must maintain a judicial approach. The intermingling of criminal- and exclusively welfare-orientated civil proceedings into one court serves to compound this confusion in the eyes of all. In some courts children awaiting civil care proceedings have to mix with police officers and young offenders. Little wonder that some of these children believe they have done wrong, especially when they later meet young offenders at their children's or community home and find that they are there on the same kind of order – a care order.

Such injustices are part of the contradictory policies which underlie dealing with children in trouble. This book looks critically at our current approaches and suggests new procedures. The first part (primarily written by Allison Morris and Henri Giller) is concerned with delinquent children; the second (primarily written by Elizabeth Szwed and Hugh Geach) with abused and neglected children. In recommending distinct criminal and family courts we seek to acknowledge the differences between these children and to eradicate current confusions.

We set out and elaborate the principles on which such systems should be based. They are by no means exhaustive and their precise formulation is open to debate. This manifesto for action includes compromises between ideological beliefs and social realities, but these compromises are peripheral to our main principle: the limitation of compulsory state intervention in the lives of children. Our proposals are not a legitimation of a laissez-faire approach towards social inequalities. The helping services – education, welfare, health – have the responsibility of assisting those who experience difficulties in their daily lives. Limiting compulsory intervention means the corresponding expansion of voluntary services. Nor are our proposals in respect of delinquent children a mandate for the punitive policies of the 'law and order' lobby. Compulsory intervention in the lives of children must be limited in nature, not subject to indiscriminate intervention on the basis of current moral panics. The judicial system has only a limited role to play in the socialisation of children. Our aim is to provide justice for children.

Part I
Crime and Justice

1
The Juvenile Court in Action: Practice and Panics

> It is an unhappy fact that criminals are getting younger and younger, and that the offences committed by juveniles are becoming more and more serious. The police, and most magistrates, believe that the existing law, the Children and Young Persons Act 1969, is proving itself to be incapable of dealing with rising juvenile criminality. The Act has, it is argued, allowed young offenders to commit crimes with virtual impunity: and by placing the emphasis on the treatment and care of delinquents, rather than on deterrence or punishment, freed persistent child criminals to carry on their nefarious activities (*The Times*, 10 July 1978).

This editorial from *The Times* typifies much of the current anxiety surrounding the Children and Young Persons Act 1969. Juvenile crime, it is claimed, has reached 'epidemic proportions'; it is also said that children 'are encouraged to become criminals' and that young offenders 'deride the powerlessness of the courts to do anything effective'. Has this 'moral panic' a basis in reality? To what extent can the 1969 Children and Young Persons Act really be blamed for this situation? This chapter seeks to answer these questions, but first looks at the philosophy behind the current legislation and examines what the proponents of the 1969 Act intended to achieve.

Towards social welfare

The Children Act 1908 set out for the first time the principle that young offenders should be heard separately from adults, and established juvenile courts – special sittings of the magistrates' courts. In essence they functioned as criminal courts and the mode of trial was the same as it was for adults. The prevailing idea was that the child was a wrongdoer and the old procedures for dealing with adult offenders were thought to be appropriate in most respects for dealing with children. In addition, though the courts were given a wide and flexible range of dispositions – discharge, fine, probation and removal from home – determination of these was governed by such considerations as the seriousness of the offence and the interest of the public.

The courts remained like this until 1933, when certain changes were made: the appointment of justices with a special interest in children, restrictions on the reporting of cases in newspapers, the abolition of the terms 'conviction' and 'sentence' and the direction that justices should have regard to the welfare of the child. These changes meant that at the adjudicative stage the delinquent act was viewed as an act of conscious defiance, but that after the act was proved or admitted it was viewed as a product of personal or external forces. This ambivalence was reflected in the various dispositions the court could impose. On the one hand, an expanding range of punishments were made available to the juvenile courts (e.g. detention centres and attendance centres); on the other, the child care service became increasingly concerned with delinquent children (for example, through fit person orders).

These ideas of criminal justice and welfare were not logically compatible, and were identified as the major weakness in the operation of the juvenile court by the Ingleby Committee in 1960. But the proposals of the Committee did little to remedy this. The subsequent Children and Young Persons Act 1963 merely raised the age of criminal responsibility from 8 to 10. Section 1 emphasised the need for preventive work with children and their families, but few resources were committed to this.

Also in the early 1960s the Labour Party sought to rethink the role of the criminal law in relation to children and produced a series of White Papers – *Child, Family and Young Offender* in 1965 and *Children in Trouble* in 1968. Underlying the proposals was the belief that delinquency was often a normal part of growing up and that criminal proceedings were inappropriate where delinquency was trivial. The existing machinery of the law was said to be reserved for working-class children; middle-class children were dealt with informally (through schools, psychiatric services etc.). Serious delinquency, on the other hand, was seen as evidence of the need for help and guidance. Criminal proceedings in such cases were said to be indefensible; what was needed was the application of the necessary treatment without the stigma of a criminal court appearance. In these cases the causes of juvenile delinquency, like child neglect, were traced to a primary source: inadequacy or breakdown in the family. Delinquency was evidence of the lack of care, guidance and opportunities which parents should provide. The child who offended was assumed to have 'needs' which could be 'diagnosed', 'treated' and eventually 'cured'. Protecting society from delinquency and helping the delinquent child's development were seen as complementary. Merely to sanction the child for his criminal acts was inappropriate; as a consequence, the juvenile court was to perform a radically different role – enabling the child to receive the help he required. The exact form and content of that help was to be left to those with specialist skills, and the order providing such help had to be of sufficient length to enable the child to be properly treated. When circumstances changed, different treatments were to be tried.

These principles were embodied in the Children and Young Persons Act 1969. Though the formal composition and constitution of the juvenile court were left virtually unchanged, its jurisdiction was radically altered. Children under the age of 14 were not to be referred to the juvenile court solely on the ground that they had committed offences. Rather, where it could be established that such children were not receiving the care, protection and guidance a good parent might reasonably be expected to give, it was proposed that 'care and protection' proceedings should be brought. Criminal proceedings would be possible against children between the ages of 14 and 17 who had committed offences, but only after mandatory consultation had taken place between the police and social services departments. The expectation was that such children would also, in the main, be dealt with under 'care and protection' proceedings.

The general aims of the Act were to reduce the number of children appearing before the juvenile court and to make the commission of an offence no longer a sufficient ground for intervention. The juvenile court was not only to become a *welfare* providing agency, but was also to become an agency of *last resort*: referral to the juvenile court was to take place only where a voluntary and informal agreement could not be reached between social workers, the child and his parents.

Integral to these proposals was the creation of an enlarged and significant role for local-authority social workers. In addition to mandatory social-work consultations before court proceedings and to increased social work with families and children on a voluntary basis, considerable power was also placed in the hands of social workers to vary and implement the dispositions made by the courts. Magistrates were no longer to make detailed decisions about the kind of treatment appropriate for the child. Social workers, within the limits of the particular order, were to determine this. Attendance centres and detention centres were to be replaced by a new form of treatment – intermediate treatment – and the form which this would take would also lie with the social services.

The treatment was called 'intermediate' because it was meant to lie between supervision at home and committal to care. It fell into two categories. The first comprised temporary residence, attendance or participation for periods not exceeding one month during each year of supervision. The aim here was to bring the young person into contact with a new environment or activity – to provide a means for broadening his experience in ways likely to be beneficial to his development as an individual and as a member of society. An essential aspect was that it would give the child the type of experiences and activities which were available in the community for *other* children. The second category called for residence at a specified place for a fixed period of not more than three months. This type of treatment would be available when the basic need was for help in the home but where a short period away from home was felt to be desirable. Approved schools were to be merged with other residential institutions (e.g. children's homes) within a single system of community homes and local authorities were to develop a wide range of facilities for children in need. Care orders, which were to replace approved school and fit person orders, vested parental rights over children with the local authority until they were 18.

In practice this model has never come to fruition; to a large extent the Act is still a non-Act. The juvenile courts function very much as before. Ideological differences between the political parties caused key sections of the Act to remain unimplemented. Criminal proceedings for offenders under 14 have not been prohibited nor have they been restricted in the case of offenders between the age of 14 and 17. Similarly the minimum age qualification for a borstal sentence has not been increased from 15 to 17, and detention centres and attendance centres have not been phased out.

Practice . . .

Nevertheless it is clear that the Act could have been implemented *informally* had the various professional groups so desired. For example, the police and social workers could have consulted each other more, but they have not. Even the implemented sections have had minimal impact. Care proceedings on the commission of an offence are now possible, but between 1971 (the year the Act was partially implemented) and 1977 the number actually decreased. The traditional 'punitive' disposals, which were to have been abolished, are increasingly used by juvenile courts. Intermediate treatment schemes – designed to keep children out of institutions – have not been fully developed and, furthermore, supervision in the community is used only slightly more now by juvenile courts than was probation before the Act. In all, the distribution of measures used by the juvenile court indicates that there has been little change in the direction intended.

Even where new agencies have been developed, they have not always met expectations. For example, despite the increase in the number of boys cautioned by the police for indictable (serious) offences between 1971 and 1977 (58 per cent), the number proceeded against in the juvenile courts has continued to increase. Before 1969 many police forces made little use of cautioning. With the passing of the Act, the practice of cautioning juveniles was encouraged and, as a result, the majority of police areas established juvenile bureaux to make the decision whether or not to refer particular children to the juvenile courts. It was intended that juvenile bureaux should keep children out of court wherever possible, but figures from the annual criminal statistics suggest that this has not happened. Although the cautioning rate for boys under 14 rose by 54 per cent between 1971 and 1977 (from 27,389 to 42,154), only 472 fewer were found guilty of indictable offences (21,401 compared with 20,929). At the same time, the number of boys from 14 to 17 found guilty of indictable offences rose from 43,789 to 62,639, despite an increase in the cautioning figure for this age group by 63 per cent (20,160 to 32,901).

It is possible that this phenomenon is due to a vast increase in juvenile crime; but Ditchfield's research suggests that at least part of the reason for this is that the pool of officially labelled juvenile offenders has increased as a direct result of changes in police practices since 1969. In addition, given that the majority of bureaux take juveniles to court automatically when a further offence has been committed, it is not surprising that the juvenile court population continues to rise despite the increased use of police cautioning.

. . . and panics

Despite these limitations, the Act has been described as a failure. A closer look at some of these developments shows how the 'moral panic' about delinquent youth is sustained. The 1969 Act has been blamed for vast increases in juvenile crime. Recorded juvenile crime did increase by 37 per cent between 1971 and 1977, but such increases are not restricted to juveniles. Recorded adult crime also increased at a comparable rate – by 25 per cent. There are, however, problems in relying upon official records to make statements about increases in the crime rate.

Because of the 'dark figure' of crime, that is crime which is unrecorded and unreported, it is impossible to say to what extent there has been a real increase in juvenile crime. We have no idea of the relation between the actual amount of crime committed and the crime which becomes known to the police. It may well be that since the partial implementation of the 1969 Act the amount of actual crime has been increasing at the same rate as recorded crime and that the 'dark figure' of juvenile crime has remained constant. But, equally, this proportion could have varied and actual crime could, in fact, have fallen. It is impossible to make exact statements.

Certainly self-report studies (i.e. studies based on self-admissions by samples of schoolchildren of their criminal behaviour) and victim studies (i.e. studies based on self-admissions by victims of criminal behaviour) do show that the 'dark figure' is sufficiently large to cast doubt on statistics based on the number of offences known to the police. Belson's survey of 1,400 London boys between the age of 13 and 16 shows that more than one-third had stolen property of one kind or another. While many of the acts admitted were of a trivial nature, there were a substantial number of boys who were officially non-delinquent but who had committed relatively serious offences. Interviews with victims have shown similar results. Sparks' research of victims in three areas of London revealed that less than one-tenth of the crimes committed in the survey areas had been reported to the police. Furthermore, McCabe's research in Oxford shows that many crimes reported to the police are not subsequently recorded by them for a variety of reasons (for example, the matter was better dealt with through other mechanisms). Despite methodological problems with these types of studies, they do alert us to the importance of realising that the recording of an event in the criminal statistics is the outcome of a sequence of social and psychological processes.

First, the event must be *perceived* by someone: property must be missed. Next, the person who perceives the event must *define* it: for example, the property must be viewed as misplaced, borrowed or stolen. Assuming that it is defined as an illegal act, the witness must then decide whether or not to *report* it to the police. He may decide not to do so perhaps through fear or embarrassment. If he does notify the police, a separate process of redefinition takes place, since the police may take a very different view of 'what happened'. Finally, where the police do define the event as illegal, they still have some discretion whether or not to record it in the criminal statistics.

The criminal statistics, therefore, represent a partial and imperfect representation of the world of crime. The statistics for 1977 show that juveniles under 17 committed 50 per cent of recorded burglaries, 38 per cent of recorded thefts, 33 per cent of recorded criminal damage and 30 per cent of recorded robberies. But these are not 'true' figures; at the very least, we must bear in mind that only 41 per cent of offences are cleared up by the police. Young people may be grossly over-represented in our crime figures. Throughout the centuries they have been perceived as social problems; they serve as a metaphor for the frustrations and fears of the older generation. General anxieties about 'stability', 'permissiveness' and 'immorality' are often reflected in discussions about juvenile crime. Young people are seen as rejecting traditional values, and become a focus for these wider concerns. The visibility and vulnerability of young people provide a forum within which these anxieties can be expressed. The stereotype of 'the hooligan', 'the vandal' and the 'deprived child' not only reflect issues about the quality of social life in general, but also serve to focus attention on certain areas and groups. Children are a highly visible section of our population and their criminal activities, often spontaneously and ineptly executed, are under the constant scrutiny of the adult world. A self-fulfilling prophecy is created: these concerns become 'real' and these individuals become 'problems'.

Nevertheless it is the way in which we perceive a situation which determines our views and attitudes towards it. Criminal statistics are not presented with cautious caveats about their interpretation – they are presented as 'facts'. Given the belief that juvenile crime has dramatically increased, it is not surprising that the powers of the juvenile court have become a central issue in discussions about the 1969 Act. Lack of informal implementation is rationalised by the magistracy as an attempt to curb what is seen, by them, as an increasing spiral of lawlessness. Hence, between 1971 and 1977 there has been an increase of 70 per cent in the number of boys given attendance centre orders and an increase of 225 per cent in the number of juveniles sent to detention centres. Similarly the number of borstal recommendations made by juvenile court magistrates increased by 52 per cent. Meanwhile, of those new measures introduced by the 1969 Act, care orders have declined in use – by 19 per cent – and the number of supervision orders has increased only slightly – by 3 per cent. The opposite to that intended by the 1969 Act has occurred and, paradoxically, the Act is blamed for this.

But examination of sentencing patterns over a longer period of time reveals that responsibility for these trends cannot be laid entirely at the foot of the new legislation. The use of probation was already decreasing from at least 1964 onwards for those under 14 and it was used *more frequently* for the older age group at various periods after 1971 than before. It also shows that the 'dramatic' increase in the use of detention centres, attendance centres and recommendations to the Crown Court for borstal training is not what it seems at first sight. The use of these measures was increasing steadily throughout the period 1964 to 1977, and in certain years before 1971 the rate of increase was as high as that since 1971. Sentencing patterns have not changed since the Act; the practice of the juvenile court has continued much as before. But, again, it is *believed* that the situation has changed – indeed, has become worse.

We are not seeking here to minimise the increases which have occurred in the absolute number of children in detention centres and borstals, but rather to suggest that alternative methods of interpretation are possible. Currently magistrates and police point to the increased detention centre population as evidence for the existence of a 'hard-core' of persistent offenders; social workers use the same figures as evidence of the failure of magistrates to work within the philosophy of the Act. Magistrates have responded by pointing to their lack of confidence in social workers as the reason for not placing children in the supervision or care of local authorities.

The 'moral panic' which surrounds present discussions about the 1969 Act is, in part, a purposeful construct by those who seek to wield power within the juvenile justice system. By presenting juvenile delinquency as problematic, each group is able to criticise the existing machinery and to promote its proposals for reform. Meanwhile, in the midst of this political power-play, thousands of children are processed through the juvenile justice system every year.

2
The Juvenile Court in Action: Conflict and Crisis

Conflict surrounding the 1969 Act is not new. During the parliamentary debates on the Bill, bitter wrangles occurred on party political lines. The Act is the product of the Labour Party's 1968 White Paper *Children in Trouble*. Before this, however, in 1964, the Labour Party had set up a committee on criminal policy under the chairmanship of Lord Longford. The report was fairly wide-ranging and a major proposal was the abolition of the juvenile courts. An alternative framework was suggested: a 'family service' in which the child, family and social worker could discuss the treatment of the child. Only where agreement could not be reached or where the facts of the case were disputed would the case be referred to a new 'family court'.

These proposals subsequently formed the basis of the Labour Government's 1965 White Paper *The Child, the Family and the Young Offender*, except that a 'family council' consisting of social workers and other persons selected for their understanding and experience of children replaced the 'family service'. There was considerable opposition to these proposals; the main criticisms centred on the inappropriateness of a treatment approach towards children who offend. Politically, the Conservative Party and, professionally, the probation service and the magistracy expressed considerable concern about the lack of protection of the legal rights of the child. They felt that there were too many possibilities for abuse in the proposed scheme and it was undesirable that decisions which might affect the liberty of the young should be reached by social workers. The need for a judicial assessment of guilt or innocence was said to outweigh consideration of treatment 'needs'.

It was in response to this opposition that the Government

produced a second White Paper, *Children in Trouble*, in 1968, which was an attempt to retain the proposals of the earlier White Paper and, at the same time, to forestall further criticism. This was achieved by abandoning the controversial 'family council' concept and by retaining the juvenile court. The opposition was thereby deprived of much of its sting, though the Conservative Party did voice major reservations about the proposals. Raising the age of criminal responsibility to 14 was strongly resisted; individual responsibility was a fundamental tenet of the Conservative Party's policy. Similarly it argued that the need to prove that children lacked care and control in addition to proof of the commission of a criminal offence put working-class children and parents at a disadvantage. (This argument that the Act was biased against working-class children proved difficult for Labour ministers to counteract.) When the Labour Government fell in 1970, it was not surprising that the new Conservative Government did not implement key sections of the Act.

Ideological conflict: 'the world as is'

Proponents of the Act assumed that those asked to participate in the operation of the Act shared a common view of the appropriate way of handling children who offend. What was ignored was that while each group may share a long-term goal – let us say the prevention of delinquent behaviour – there is little agreement about the best *method* of achieving this objective. Because the Act was only implemented in part, groups which found their role in conflict with others have been able to continue to work within their traditional perspectives. In addition, individual groups may have immediate objectives which conflict with the immediate objectives of other key agencies. For example, the Police Federation wrote: 'We are fundamentally concerned with the protection of the public, the prevention of crime, and the detection of offenders. Our concern in the treatment of offenders is therefore considered in the light of the above principles' (Police Federation, 1975, p. 287). This is, of course, what the public expect of the police. The point is that it is not a view which is widely held by social workers. For example, the British Association of Social Workers stated that 'for most juvenile offenders the stigma of criminality is inappropriate and help can best be provided through the educational and social services within the community without recourse to a court appearance' (BASW, 1975, p. 211). It is not surprising, therefore, that tension between the police and social workers has arisen.

Similarly magistrates have argued in favour of 'equality before the law', have complained that the powers of the court have been abrogated and that the lives and liberty of children have been entrusted to the executive. These views clearly clash with the new role of local-authority social workers – the executive. Rather than 'equality before the law', which demands similar dispositions for similar conduct by similar people, social workers recommend and implement dispositions based on the maxim 'to each according to his needs' – they see the child's conduct as only one manifestation of the totality of his make-up, which has little place of itself in determining the appropriate disposition.

Often there is an *apparent* congruence in the working ideologies of the various groups. Individual groups, for example, may refer to the 'welfare of the child', but often each means something quite different; the congruence is superficial. Magistrates and police feel that it is not in the interests of a child subject to a care order to be able to commit further offences without encountering additional penalties. Social workers, on the other hand, feel that it is not in the child's interests to refer him on *every* occasion to the court – they may prefer to continue to work with the child despite his further delinquency.

Another example is apparent agreement that further 'resources' are necessary to make the Act work. Magistrates have asked for 'some kind of "long-stop" measure' so that young offenders 'are shown that in the last resort the law has teeth' (Magistrates' Association, 1975, p. 463). Social workers, on the other hand, have asked for more resources in the form of increased manpower and social service budgets. The euphemisms 'resources' and 'welfare' conceal these incongruities.

The continuing debate on whether or not the care order is an adequate mechanism for dealing with troublesome children is an example of these conflicts and tensions. From the outset it was clear that the imposition of a care order by the juvenile court was not meant necessarily to remove the child from his home. What was intended was that local-authority social workers would have the power to do so if they believed this was in the child's best interests. The intention was to separate the judicial function of magistrates from the treatment function of social workers. However, many magistrates believe that the care order is a residential order and that the failure of social workers to remove children from their homes after such a disposition is an arbitrary flouting of their wishes. For example, one juvenile court magistrate (quoted in an article in the *Magistrate*) said:

> We feel frustrated. We feel we have done the best for the children and sent them away from home. Then we see them walking along the road looking at the magistrates, shouting 'ha, ha, we've won, you have lost' (*Magistrate*, 1974, vol. 30, no. 11, p. 168).

Moreover magistrates believe that leaving children subject to care orders in their own homes exacerbates their propensity to re-offend and makes them impervious to the influence of the courts. This, they claim, has created a 'minority' of tough sophisticated young criminals who prey on the community at will and deride the powerlessness of the court. But empirical evidence about the 'ineffectiveness' of care orders is sparse. The little evidence which does exist contradicts the impression that children are automatically sent home (or run away) and commit further offences.

Care orders invariably involve placing children in institutions for some period of time. Usually there is an initial placement for between 6 weeks and 3 months for 'diagnosis' of the child's 'problems' in an observation and assessment centre. In surveys of 20 local authorities during 1972 and 1973 the Social Work Service Division of the DHSS found that it was comparatively rare for children subject to care orders to be returned home directly from court. This was confirmed by Cawson's 1975 survey, which found that 31 per cent of children subject to care orders were initially placed in observation and assessment centres. The reasons given for allowing children home included 'home conditions improved and thought able to cope with the child' and 'the child's removal from home thought to be unnecessary or unsuitable'.

Zander's study of a small sample of London children subject to care orders showed that, while a high proportion of children were returned home, this was not inevitably associated with further offences. Those children placed in a community home in fact committed *more* offences subsequently than those placed at home (including those for whom no residential place was available). This is again confirmed by Cawson's research. Just over one-third of her sample committed another offence during the 9-month period following the making of the care order, but more than two-thirds of them were in residential care at the time of the offence. Very few children placed at home committed a second offence. But belief in the need for residence in an institution following the imposition of a care order and in the myth that approved school orders (which were automatically residential) were effective in preventing absconding and recidivism remain strong. In fact approved schools had a reconviction rate of around 65 per cent and absconding rose annually despite decreases in the approved-school population. Whether these impressions are fact or fiction is probably irrelevant; they have been formed and affect the operation of the Act. This perceived lack of effective powers was said by the Secretary of the Magistrates' Association to force courts to send young people *who might not otherwise be sent there* to detention centres and borstals.

Much of this ideological conflict has become transmuted into indignation at the real or imagined defects of the various professional groups. Take magistrates' stereotypes of social workers. First, they question their *personal* characteristics. The comments of Baroness Macleod (a juvenile court magistrate) in a House of Lords debate illustrate this:

> We are aware that many social work staff are very immature and inexperienced; many have themselves been brought up in schools and houses without any discipline, and often without respect for and belief in law and order (quoted in *Justice of the Peace*, 1977, p. 141).

By this technique magistrates can then question the *professional* competence of social workers. Two quotations by magistrates from a book by Berlins and Wansell provide examples of this:

> The young social worker, who to some of us looks no different from the children themselves, is often just not up to coping with difficult children (Berlins and Wansell, 1974, p. 82).
>
> How can these young people, fresh from university departments of sociology, but otherwise completely untrained and inexperienced, possibly understand the needs of a delinquent child from a deprived home in one of the city's slums? (Berlins and Wansell, 1974, p. 85).

But reverse this: 'How can these middle-aged, middle-class people, virtually untrained, who customarily sit in adult courts meting out punishment, possibly understand . . . ?' Of course, neither picture is real, but stereotyping has important ideological functions; it not only tells us 'how the world *is*' but also, by implication, suggests to us '*how the world ought to be*'.

Ideological conflict: 'the world as ought'

Indicative of this divergence of perspectives is the fact that as early as 1974 a sub-committee of the House of Commons Expenditure Committee was established to review this whole area (see House of Commons Expenditure Committee, 1975, in Bibliography). The appointment of the sub-committee provided a convenient forum for the various parties to state their case and present their recommendations for the future. The evidence submitted to the sub-committee fell into four broad categories. First there was the 'radical' view that the 1969 Act did not go far enough. The National Council for Civil Liberties, for example, felt that 'the roots of juvenile crime and thus measures to combat it are to be found in the social and physical environment'. Urgent attention required to be focused on 'bad housing, poor planning, schools' and the 'lack of opportunities for acceptable achievements'. The second view was that of 'crime control': the Act was based on unsound principles. The Justices' Clerks' Society, for example, said that the Act failed because it blurred the distinction between a child in need of care and a child offender, and because it deprived society of 'an important part of the criminal court's jurisdiction, namely, to protect the public'. The third view was the 'child care' view, which accepted the broad principles of the Act and called for full implementation. Thus the British Association of Social Workers argued that the Act provided 'a legal structure for dealing with juvenile delinquency which is both enlightened and appropriate without substantial amendment'. The final view was the 'crime control/child care' view, which suggested that children in trouble might be susceptible to child care but that some required penal measures regardless of this susceptibility. The Magistrates' Association, for example, felt that for most children the Act had worked quite well but that 'for a minority of tough sophisticated young criminals . . . it had been disastrous'.

Faced with these conflicting views, the sub-committee attempted a compromise but was heavily influenced by the 'crime control/child care' view. Its report contained 40 recommendations in all, many of which were directed towards the smooth running of the Act and covered minor administrative changes (e.g. social workers should be trained in court procedure). A few recommendations substantially reinforced the treatment philosophy underlying the Act (e.g. the development of non-residential forms of care). But the most far-reaching recommendations were those which represented a movement away from this philosophy: the sub-committee recommended the return to magistrates of powers thought to be inappropriate in the 1968 White Paper and in the 1969 Act. These recommendations were that:

1. when a care order is made, magistrates and social workers should agree in court on what should be done with the child;
2. when a juvenile already subject to a care order appears before a court charged with an offence, the court should be able to impose a secure care order;
3. attendance and detention centres should be retained; and
4. probation officers rather than social workers should deal with children who offend.

These recommendations sought to remedy what was seen as the major failing of the 1969 Act: 'It is not wholly effective in differentiating between children who need care, welfare, better education and mere support from society and the small minority who need strict control and an element of punishment.' This statement rejects the notion that the 'depraved' and the 'deprived' are one and the same, and suggests rather the existence of the 'acceptable depraved' (minor or first offenders) and the 'unacceptable depraved' (serious or persistent offenders).

The Government responded to these recommendations in an inter-departmental White Paper published in May of 1976. Basically this White Paper (Home Office, Welsh Office, etc., 1976) failed to take a firm stand in the determination of future juvenile court policy, reflected confused thinking and made disparate recommendations. The observations begin in a vein consistent with the philosophy of the 1969 Act. However, also in the introduction, there are statements of equal force yet opposite intent. It supports, for example, the sub-committee's belief that there exists a minority of serious and persistent offenders identifiable by the nature of their behaviour. This strikes at the root of the philosophy underlying the 1969 Act. *Children in Trouble* stated that dispositions should 'be soundly based on the best possible diagnosis of the *child's needs* and circumstances'. This reaffirms the creation of two separate systems of dealing with juvenile offenders: one based on minor or inconsequential offending and the other on serious or persistent offending.

The unquestioning continuation of detention centres also showed that the intention of the Act was long forgotten. Likewise, attendance centres were to be expanded as soon as conditions permitted. Indeed, the expansion of attendance centres summed up the White Paper's approach. They combined the magical duality of 'an easily understood punishment' with teaching 'the boys something of a constructive use of leisure'. In short, control and care were intertwined.

In one major area, however, the White Paper was not prepared to go as far as the sub-committee's report. It explicitly accepted and reaffirmed the different functions of juvenile court magistrates and social workers: judicial and treatment. Yet the White Paper went on to give magistrates a power to recommend, in those cases which caused them concern, what should be done with a child – for example, placement of a child subject to a care order in a secure institution. By giving magistrates this power to recommend certain dispositions, the White Paper seemed to assume that magistrates and social workers had the same view of the 'needs' of the child. Yet earlier in the document it had accepted that they did not. The White Paper attempted to please all and pleased none.

Concealed consensus

As a result of this White Paper, a joint working party consisting of representatives from the Magistrates' Association, the local authorities' associations and the DHSS was established to develop a common code of practice for the operation of the Act. The resulting report comments that on a number of issues there were major differences of opinion between magistrates and local authorities. There was, however, some agreement on, for example, the existence of a 'hard-core' of juvenile offenders; but the various representatives disagreed on the best method of dealing with this supposed 'hard-core'.

The magistrates' proposals restated their belief in the 'crime control/child care' view which had been presented to the House of Commons sub-committee three years previously. While accepting the philosophy of the Act for the majority of juvenile offenders, they once again proposed a 'residential care order' for the 'minority' of children who offend again after a care order has been made. While this proposal seemed more 'liberal' than previous calls for secure care orders, there were several indications that this was not so. For example, the length of residence would not be determined by legislation, but by the courts themselves. Moreover such an order was explicitly stated to represent the court's desire 'that the interests of society should at least for the time take precedence over the developmental needs of the child' and magistrates' belief that children would be deterred by such an order. It is highly unlikely, however, that these intentions could be fulfilled merely by placing a child in an open community home.

But, more significantly, the establishment of such a power would not ensure that only a minority of juvenile offenders would be subject to these 'tougher' measures. The criteria by which a child would become eligible for a residential care order were stated to be the commission of 'a further serious offence or offences such as to make it clear that he is a danger to the public, that the welfare authorities cannot control him, and that no other course is appropriate'. These subjective standards could lead to an increase in the number of children placed in custody. The 'minority' would then become the 'majority'.

In 1977 5,355 children were made the subject of a care order by juvenile court magistrates. Assume that 66 per cent of these children offend again (the last recorded success rate for approved schools) – some 3,560 children – all of them would be eligible for a residential care order within the Magistrates' Association's proposals. It takes little imagination to see that residential care orders would soon be seen as ineffective, that further powers would be demanded and that more institutions (including secure provision) would have to be built for an increasing number of children.

The local authority associations' rejection of the magistrates' proposals in principle was not based on the need to limit intervention into the lives of children. For them, 'the key to progress in dealing with the persistent young offender [is] the provision of a wider range of treatment options than is already available'. They argued for *earlier* intervention over *more* children for *longer* periods. The local authority associations' code would also result, in practice, in the increased use of residential institutions, because it suggests that if a child is living at home when additional serious offences are committed, this *in itself* indicates that he should be cared for away from home. While the language of 'needs' and 'treatment' is different from 'protection of the community' and 'deterrence', the outcome is the same.

A similar strategy is apparent in a recent set of guidelines published by the British Association of Social Workers (BASW, 1977). Although this document suggests that social workers should not recommend detention centre sentences at all or borstal orders for 15-year-olds, it goes on to specify situations in which care orders should be recommended. The import of this document is that social workers can *control* these children *as effectively* as detention centres and borstals.

Towards a consensus of control?

Despite apparent conflict among the various professionals in the juvenile justice system, 143,854 children were processed through the juvenile courts in 1977. Ideological conflict has, to a large extent, remained at the level of rhetoric because conflict can only affect practice where one group has the power and resources to enforce its beliefs in a distinctive manner.

As magistrates determine the proportion of offenders who are allocated to the social services, they have this power. Social workers, in order to maintain their credibility, have been forced to state that they can fulfil the social control function demanded by magistrates (and police). In effect a bifurcation of juvenile offenders has been created: the 'majority' of children are satisfactorily accommodated by existing (including social service) provisions and a 'minority' of hard-core offenders (characterised by their psychiatrically abnormal features or by their repeated delinquent behaviour) require additional measures of control (residential care orders, secure care orders, etc.)

Indicative of this is the growth in the number of secure places available within the community home system. Whereas 60 secure places existed in 1969, there were 212 such places by April 1977, with a further 265 places planned or under construction. Euphemisms such as 'intensive care units' or 'youth treatment centres' do not disguise the real nature of such places: control. Yet research has established that delinquent children in the 1970s are not more difficult or dangerous than those appearing before the juvenile courts in the 1960s. The expansion of secure places tells us far more about the professional interests of those who seek to control juvenile delinquency than it does about the behaviour they seek to control.

3

Treatment in Trouble

> Juvenile delinquency has no single cause, manifestation or cure. Its origins are many, and the range of behaviour which it covers is equally wide. At some points it merges almost imperceptibly with behaviour which does not contravene the law. A child's behaviour is influenced by genetic, emotional and intellectual factors, his maturity, and his family, school, neighbourhood and wider social setting. It is probably a minority of children who grow up without ever misbehaving in ways which may be contrary to the law. Frequently, such behaviour is no more than an incident in the pattern of a child's normal development. But sometimes it is a response to unsatisfactory family or social circumstances, a result of boredom in and out of school, an indication of maladjustment or immaturity, or a symptom of a deviant, damaged or abnormal personality. Early recognition and full assessment are particularly important in these more serious cases (Home Office, 1968, p. 3).

This quotation from *Children in Trouble* illustrates the philosophy which underlies the 1969 Act: a philosophy of treatment. Such an approach is not new; it has permeated the history of youth control in this country since the beginning of this century. What is new is that the 1969 Act sought to implement such a philosophy across the whole spectrum of juvenile misconduct. The treatment approach carries with it certain assumptions and in this chapter we seek to elucidate these and to question their validity.

The assumptions of treatment

The basic assumptions are, in short:

1. 'troublesome' behaviour and 'misconduct'* have antecedent causes which explain them: past conditions and situations are emphasised, individual choice is ignored;
2. these causes can be (and have been) discovered;
3. their discovery has made possible the treatment and control of such behaviour;
4. 'troublesome' children share pathological conditions which make them fundamentally different from the law-abiding;
5. 'trouble' or 'misconduct' gets 'worse' without 'treatment';
6. 'treatment' has no harmful side effects;
7. involuntary 'treatment' is not punishment.

In essence, 'misconduct' is seen as a medical problem, a social illness which can be made the subject of 'diagnosis', 'treatment', and 'cure'. 'Delinquents', 'truants', 'runaways' and other 'problem' children are seen as 'different'. But many of these assumptions are based on an over-optimistic and inadequate view of our knowledge of 'misconduct'.

The personalisation of causes

The White Paper preceding the 1969 Act endorsed a particular model of causation: it assumed that the causes of 'trouble' lay primarily within the individual and his family. These causes were said to be identified not only in overt signs of family disturbance – death, divorce, mental illness – but also within families which seemed outwardly stable. But most research has singularly failed to demonstrate empirically that certain characteristics do clearly distinguish the 'troublesome' from the 'non-troublesome'. The various studies on the effect of individual or family influences have been far from

* These concepts are used interchangeably in this chapter to include delinquency, truancy and children in moral danger. Much of the following discussion also applies to 'abused' and 'neglected' children; however, the 'trouble' or 'misconduct' in these situations is seen as the responsibility of the parents rather than the children.

convincing. Often statements have been made on the basis of samples which are not representative (e.g. adjudicated, hospitalised or institutionalised children) and now research questions this reliance on the family. For example, a recently completed study designed to investigate 45 hypotheses on causal factors in the development of stealing by adolescent boys found little evidence for the commonly alleged influence of such factors as 'broken homes' and 'parental control over spare time'. There is also now a substantial body of literature which questions the deleterious effect on child development of Bowlby's notion of 'maternal deprivation'. Furthermore, Michael Power found in a sample of boys appearing before London juvenile courts that two-thirds came from ordinary families, intact and without serious problems. This is not to say that family influences are irrelevant in understanding 'trouble', but rather that we are not able to specify what to look for or what to do about it.

Reliance on the family as the breeding ground of 'trouble' is not new. The family's failure to socialise its children was the justification for intervention in the lives of children used by nineteenth-century reformers. But whereas at that time poverty was seen as the major factor in this moral vacuum, this was not the case in the twentieth century. Against a background of social and economic post-war prosperity, troublesome children were seen as the product of 'secondary' poverty – maternal deprivation, family breakdown, large families, lack of support of the extended family – which prevented social participation. By providing these families with assistance, primarily through social services intervention, it was believed that children and their families would be able to play their full role in society and that 'troublesomeness' would disappear.

Acceptance that 'misconduct' lies primarily within the individual and his family limits the possibility of alternative explanations and reactions. The 'personalisation' of the causes of 'troublesome' behaviour means that the social reality of 'trouble' (the political and economic realities which govern relationships between man and society) can be ignored. Theorists who saw the causes of 'trouble' in the family, in inherited pathology or in class differences are all guilty of this. This 'victim blaming' allows 'troublesome' children to become categorised and stigmatised as 'different' and at the same time justifies humanitarian efforts to 'cure' their 'problems'.

By treating 'misconduct' as a problem of individual adjustment rather than, for example, a problem arising out of the social (economic and political) position and condition of adolescents, subsequent action is both determined and delimited. Not only does the choice of cause affect the choice of treatment; it also affects the adequacy of that treatment. To isolate the 'troublesome' from the impact on them of socio-economic change – high unemployment rates (at their highest among the young and aggravated by what many children see as irrelevant schooling), technological advances (with the corresponding increase in routine, monotonous jobs) and housing redevelopment (with its accompanying isolation, anonymity and fragmentation of the extended family) – makes no sense.

Some may argue that social-work theory and practice have moved away from this naive and confusing reliance on family and individual characteristics, but this is true only to a limited extent. Radical social work, for example, certainly exposes the rhetoric of treatment but provides clients with little in the way of coping with social inequalities. The rhetoric of radicalism is as irrelevant to clients as the rhetoric of Freudian theory. The view that each admission into a detention centre, borstal, secure unit, or community home marks the creation of another revolutionary martyr is unlikely to appeal to those who find themselves in such institutions.

Similarly many of those who seem to adopt the psycho-social view of 'trouble' (i.e. the client's situation results from social and environmental influences) still direct their attention towards *individual* rather than social change. Recent guidelines on the social worker's role with delinquents (issued by the British Association of Social Workers) clearly illustrate this. While acknowledging the relevance of criminological theories which stress the social construction of delinquency, the report nevertheless states that it is *individual* deficiencies which identify 'career delinquents'.

Just as there is little agreement at any precise level about the underlying reasons for 'misconduct', there is little evidence that known 'treatments' for 'troublesome' behaviour – for example, supervision or institutional placements – have any rehabilitative effect. Failure in the sense of further 'trouble', conviction or reconviction is common. The reconviction rate of children leaving approved schools showed that some 66 per cent offended again within 2 years of their release. The current failure rates of borstals and detention centres are 73 per cent and 81 per cent respectively. Even such new treatment measures as intermediate treatment schemes have had little or no impact on delinquency. (Some argue that further 'trouble' or delinquency is an invalid measure of the success of 'treatment', but these reflect success or failure in other areas of life – for example, industrial life and family obligations.) There is some indication also that intervention may increase the likelihood of 'trouble'. Millham and others argue that repeated residential 'treatment' is one of the best ways of ensuring that children will continue to experience residential custody. Other detrimental effects can also result from residential 'treatment': educational progress is poor, employment prospects may be hindered, the child's self-concept may alter and he may see himself as 'troublesome'. Yet the new system was based primarily on the same resources as the old; names were changed but supervision and residential institutions continue essentially as before.

Failure rates like these must be a matter of concern because a treatment approach provides justification for early and extensive intervention in the lives of children and their families; if 'misconduct' reflects a maladjustment which can be treated, then it is wrong to restrict the availability of treatment or to deprive the child of it. 'A fence at the top of the hill rather than an ambulance at the bottom' is a recurrent metaphor used by those seeking to extend intervention. As a result, the net of control is cast wider.

Research suggests, for example, that the use of police cautioning since the implementation of the Act has meant that children previously dealt with informally are now being dealt with formally. A similar pattern had emerged in the development of intermediate treatment. Social workers have increasingly directed their intermediate treatment efforts to the 'at risk' groups – pre-delinquent, deprived children – and have not dealt with adjudicated children to the same extent. As a consequence, when children subsequently appear in the juvenile court, absolute discharge, intermediate treatment and supervision are seen as inappropriate dispositions. This means that they become subject to more incursive intervention; the imposition of care orders on young children for first offences is readily legitimated. Cawson's research, for example, shows that 31 per cent of those made subject to care orders in 1975 had no previous court appearances, and a further 28 per cent had only one court appearance. As the care order vests parental rights over children with the local authority until they are 18 and as the age of criminal responsibility remains at 10, children can receive *what they see* as an 8 year 'sentence' for a first or minor offence.

Research

The creation of trouble

The categorisation of an individual as an 'offender' or as a 'problem' is not solely the product of the commission of an act; it is also the product of the individual's interaction with others who witness the deviant act – police, social worker, school-teacher, educational welfare officer, magistrate or whoever – and who impose that social description. There is now a significant body of research on unreported delinquency and on definitions of truancy which challenges traditional accounts of 'misconduct'. Reynolds, for example, has shown that different 'truancy' rates in different schools are, in part, explained by the way in which teachers treat the children in their charge. The expectations which policemen, teachers and social workers have about children (and their power to act on them) have traditionally been ignored in the search for explanations of 'trouble'. But how 'something done' comes to be objectified as 'deviant behaviour' requiring intervention is a critical issue. Children who are brought into the system are selected along epidemiological lines: those who operate the system concentrate their attention on those whom they believe most likely to commit delinquent acts or experience 'problems'. 'Misconduct' is not merely behaviour, but the interpretation of behaviour by decision-makers. Where there are few *objective* criteria by which the nature and extent of a 'problem' can be determined, decision-makers end up by referring to their own values and beliefs, i.e. *subjective* criteria. The 'troublesome' are evaluated favourably or unfavourably not because they *do* something, not even because they *are* something, but because *others react* to their perception of them as favourable or unfavourable. Being 'beyond control' or 'exposed to moral danger' are not objective conditions; they exist when defined as such. Whether or not, for example, 'proper development is being avoidably prevented or neglected' or a child is beyond parental control is not an issue of fact; it depends upon interpretation of the parents' child-rearing practices. These, in turn, reflect wider ideologies concerning the appropriate roles of women, men, children and families within society. The assumption that children will be 'nurtured' by 'mothers' and 'fathers' is not based on biological empiricism; rather, as anthropologists have consistently demonstrated, parenthood and the demand that mothers 'nurse' children are cultural constructs.

Traditionally decision-makers have sought information to aid them in their search for 'real trouble'. The rapid expansion of observation and assessment centres since the passing of the 1969 Act epitomises the treatment ideology in practice. Assessment centres, in the name of scientific 'problem solving', serve as the prime example of the bureaucratisation of the labelling process. Such descriptions as 'personality disorder', 'psychopath' and 'dangerous' not only stigmatise children but, perforce, create expectations: the process becomes self-fulfilling. In addition, research shows that the language of 'treatment' merely obfuscates the real criteria of assessment: the age, sex and geographical location of the child and the availability of vacancies in institutions. As one American professor graphically put it, the assessment process is like a five-lane highway which leads to a dungheap!

Because we do not understand the significance of much juvenile 'misconduct', the various reports presented to decision-makers contain value judgements and unfounded assumptions. As a general rule, we do not know with certainty which factors to refer to, or which situations indicate which form of 'treatment'. Because of this, we tend to collect either information which perpetuates stereotypes of the cause of 'trouble' (broken home, working mother and so on) or all possible information in the hope or belief that something might be relevant. As such, these reports are useless guides to choosing dispositions, but these 'facts' then justify the form and content of intervention. These reports recast or reconstitute the child's identity as a 'delinquent', 'truant' or 'troublesome'. They are, in essence, what one American writer calls 'character assassinations', which seek to inculpate the child and thereby provide legitimation for greater incursion into his life than could be provided by the circumstances of the event.

The following extracts from a social inquiry report on a child (John) made the subject of a care order for a first offence of burglary illustrates several of these techniques. First the report addresses the issue of family history and constructs a genealogy of 'trouble'.

> [The step-father] was one of triplets and the two other babies died. He is the youngest child, having four sisters and one brother. He is very punitive and comes from a deprived and harsh background. He was said to have truanted from school as a child and had also been in trouble and sent to Borstal before he joined the Army when he was 17.

[The mother] has told me that her family were very close. She was very upset by the death of her parents. Her father died in 1971. Her mother died a year ago and she took over the care of the maternal grandmother. She describes her maternal grandmother as a difficult and cantankerous woman . . . [The mother] felt unable to share her feelings of loss and anger when her mother died. Her husband did not want to know. She feels that a lot of her feelings were picked up by John who has always been close to her.

The history of the boy from birth is then presented and current events are linked to the previously described 'problems':

John's truancy started after the death of his grandmother. He had not settled at secondary school, disliking the long journey and the unreliable bus service, which often made him late and for which he got detention. Episodes of stealing had occurred before this and seem to have been directed towards upsetting stepfather, i.e. selling his silver cigarette box and taking his silver coins and other money. At home, John has also shown violence towards his sisters.

Finally, the various themes are drawn together to provide a 'logical' recommendation:

[Mother] has been described as a concerned, affectionate and over-protective woman, whose loyalty seems to be divided between John and her husband. Now that John is in the assessment centre, mother has aligned herself with stepfather's views, especially as they have moved to an area where they are trying to establish a new family image. Mother uses her close attachment to John to burden him with her own problems. Stepfather opts out of family problems and John has 'lost' his own father, also his grandfather whom he loved in early childhood. He is thus without a male figure for identification. A care order will take John from a difficult home situation. He will need a great deal of help in coming to terms with the shattered relationships.

The writer of this report makes use of many of the stereotypes of 'trouble' we have already mentioned: poor family relationships, parental criminality, marital tensions, school refusal and neo-Freudian interpretations of theft. The selection of the material and its coherent presentation in a particular way makes only one response possible from the reader. Material which might contradict this interpretation of events is rarely aired. Moreover, whenever possible, other professionals are referred to in order to give further weight to the particular interpretation presented. The report cited above began with the comment: 'This report is based on Education Welfare and Child Guidance reports.' In this way stereotypes are perpetuated and selectively gathered information is presented as 'fact'. What the child has '*done*', the 'seriousness' of his behaviour, becomes irrelevant; the main concern is interpretation of *what* the child (and family) *is*.

The success of these strategies can be seen from research which has demonstrated that magistrates accept the vast majority of recommendations made to them by social workers, probation officers, psychiatrists, etc. Research also shows, however, that recommendations are often tailored to meet what the report writer knows, from his experience in court, is likely to happen anyway. The magistrates' agreement with the recommendation naturally reinforces the writer's assumptions about the appropriateness of various recommendations, and this creates what Martin Davies has called 'a closed loop system of influence'. Through this loop alliances between magistrates and social welfare professionals emerge (to the exclusion of clients).

Needs or deeds?

Frances Allen wrote some years ago that 'the language of therapy is frequently employed . . . to disguise the true state of affairs' and that it can present an 'obstacle to realistic analysis'. The language of 'help' and 'treatment' is an integral part of the 1969 Act, but while the court is directed to promote the welfare of the child, such language ignores the fact that the court's decisions perforce take place in an authoritation setting: the child is referred to the court, in the main, against his will, for what he did (or did not do). His behaviour has been seen as 'troublesome', 'disruptive' or 'threatening', and as requiring the exercise of coercive powers.

The philosophy underlying the 1969 Act sought to ignore the behaviour itself; its significance was that it was symptomatic of an underlying disorder. But was it realistic to expect that notions of delinquency and 'trouble' and the kind of considerations which usually surround them could be abolished so easily in the minds of magistrates (or, for that matter, the child or his parents) merely by the passing of an Act? Is it likely that magistrates could ignore society's attitude to children who offend or indeed society's attitude to 'troublesome' children in general? Certainly research by Priestley suggests that juvenile court magistrates look mainly to offence criteria in decision-making: information in the social background reports presented to the court tended to be incorporated within this framework as mitigating factors.

This is perhaps inevitable. Adolescents often become a focus for the frustrations and tensions of the older generation; their acts are viewed as a collective challenge to cherished values. The official processing of adolescents then takes on an almost symbolic importance – it becomes a means of maintaining the *status quo*, of providing social education and of defining acceptable boundaries to behaviour.

This extent to which conduct is relevant to decision-making is not limited to the court setting. Social workers, too, are forced into acknowledging that what they do is based upon the child's behaviour: the 'deeds' of the child become a short-hand means of describing his 'needs'. Recent research on the content of supervision confirms this. It suggests that, when supervision orders are made, the primary focus for intervention by the supervision is the 'needs' of the child and the family. There are, however, difficulties in developing relationships with these children. One experienced supervisor described his work as follows:

> He's supposed to come here to me, and he's supposed to sit here and find out what troubles him and what bothers him. Well, usually he's fairly inarticulate and however at ease I make him it's an odd situation, totally foreign to him, to sit and try to delve for very long or very often into how he feels. It's a bit artificial. So the supervision order is reduced into, very often, 'How are you?', 'Have you got a job yet?' or 'Are you going to school?', 'How's your mother?' and 'What's the fishing like?'

This means that supervisors tend to create a series of stereotyped rules in order to control the child's behaviour – for example, regular reporting to the office, holding down a job, attending school, behaving well. Moreover, to sustain the meaningfulness of the order over time (supervision orders can last up to 3 years), supervisors are forced to rely on the *deterrent* aspect of the order. As one supervisor put it:

> You have to accept it's a losing battle and it becomes a quick ten minutes in and out. Then one says, well perhaps by having to come down and see me it acts as some sort of reminder that he's been in trouble, that possibly he will be in more serious trouble next time.

Despite talk of 'treatment', 'needs' and 'adjustment', staff in residential institutions, in the main, also rely upon the *behavioural conformity* of children when deciding on major issues. As one residential social worker put it at a case review: 'He's kept his nose clean; he deserves to be sent home. He's earned his release.'

Because children in residential settings are reasonably well-behaved, staff take this for granted and develop strategies to manage everyday life on this basis. Those who do not conform are a challenge to these assumptions: they become the 'deviants', the 'problems' whose motivation has to be explained. It is in this context that the pathogenic elements of the treatment ideology are made use of. The child's behaviour is interpreted as 'symptomatic' of underlying 'maladjustment'. This use of treatment ideology in a residual manner does little to help the children. The staff, rather than acknowledge that *they* have difficulty in interacting with such children, describe the *actors* as 'difficult'. In this way the philosophy of treatment serves as a latent rationale for explaining unsuccessful remedial actions in the institutional setting. By the strategic use of 'treatment' talk, behaviour which is unacceptable but legitimate (something which institutions must tolerate) can be transformed into something 'untreatable' (a matter beyond the legitimate ambit of the school, which justifies the child's removal). This, in part, explains Tutt's recent claim that since the creation of the community home system 'there has been a disturbing reduction in the control influenced by institutions over young offenders'. Tutt compared the figures for premature departures (the 'drop out' rate) of children from approved schools (in 1966) with those from the CHEs (community homes with education on the premises) in one regional planning area (in 1974). His results show that only 58 per cent of the boys and 63 per cent of the girls completed their CHE programme, compared with 89 per cent and 94 per cent respectively amongst the approved school population. It is *these* children who are described as the 'hard-core minority'; it is also for this group that the number of secure places is continually being expanded.

But the empirical evidence which is available on secure units provides little reason for optimism in choosing this approach. Millham, after studying the population and regimes of three original closed units established in the 1960s, concluded that 'for the majority of boys, the secure units provide a brief sojourn in an expensive ante-room to the penal system'. This research also shows that children currently placed in secure accommodation do not differ markedly from those in the community home system. Generally selection for secure accommodation is associated more with the failure of previous residential placements than any distinct characteristic of the offender. These children are the 'casualties of the child-care system'. Secure units, moreover, have a high failure rate when assessed by further delinquency – 76 per cent.

Confusing the clients

Though the clients of the juvenile justice system are subjected to dispositions which are presented as being 'in their best interest', they themselves see them as punitive. In relation to delinquents, research on the former juvenile courts in England indicated that children wanted to 'get off', did not want to be 'sent away' and did not share the treatment-oriented aims of the court. They saw the juvenile court as an agency in which punishment was dealt out and were confused by dispositions which did not conform to this ideal. Recent research (by two of us) on the current juvenile courts confirms this. The results suggest that delinquent children see the role of the court as that of administering 'justice' in the traditional sense of the term: intervention justified on proof of the commission of an offence and the proportionality of sentence to offence. They expected a tariff of dispositions founded on punishment. ('The fine was too much for a first offence.') Moreover they expected penalties to reflect the offender's culpability. When co-defendants were dealt with differently, this was seen as right and fair where obvious differences could be pointed to: the existence of a previous record or greater responsibility for the current offence. When deviation from these principles was observed (e.g. when social or family background information was referred to), the children saw it as unfair. As one boy said: 'They shouldn't look at your home, they should only look at the offence. At home you don't do anything wrong. They should only look at your home if you've done something wrong there.'

We also found that communication between the child and the magistrates was in the main routine: 'What have you got to say for yourself?' 'Nothing.' The few exceptions to this were when the offence was denied and the child gave evidence. Some children expressed a fear of participation ('I didn't speak in case I got something wrong'); others felt that matters were predetermined anyway. ('You couldn't make them change their mind' or 'The magistrates knew what to do before I went in'.) The majority certainly felt that they had no influence on the outcome of the case. This impression that the court-room scene is being played out without much help from the children is confirmed by the fact that half the children in our sample could not correctly identify the magistrates. (Two young girls appearing in court for the first time identified the 'judge' [the chairman] because he had the biggest chair. When prompted about others in the room, they described the other magistrates as 'helpers in case the judge couldn't read someone's writing', and the clerk as the 'second judge'.) More than half the children could not say who had actually made the disposition decision. (Suggestions included the chairman himself, the clerk and everyone in the court room.)

Similar themes emerged from some interviews with children who were subject to supervision orders. In those cases in which co-defendants received different dispositions, this was seen as fair by the children where there were obvious differences between the co defendants. On occasions the decision was seen as unfair either because 'nothing' had happened to the co-defendant (i.e. he had been given a conditional discharge by the court) or because his sentence was seen as 'lighter' than supervision (e.g. a fine). Such comments provide further support for the view that children expect their dispositions to be based on offence and tariff criteria.

The majority of the children viewed their own supervision orders as fair. The main reason for this was that before the court hearing the children believed that the nature of their offences merited a custodial sentence; to have retained one's liberty was an unexpected dividend. Responses such as 'I thought I was lucky not to be put away' were typical. Moreover several children thought that it was the social worker or probation officer who prepared the social inquiry report who had saved them from this fate. ('If it hadn't been for my social worker, I would have been in approved school.') This opinion was often echoed by the child's parents. ('Before the case we were worried that Paul might be put away, but she said it would be probation. If she can say that before the case is heard, that's damned good guidance and it took a lot off our minds.') Of the children who saw the order as unfair, all said that this was because it did not meet their expectations of a tariff, either with respect to the seriousness of the offence ('It was only a pint of milk') or to the frequency of their delinquency ('I expected a fine for my first offence'). The supervision order, therefore, was seen by the children as occupying a particular position in a tariff of dispositions: it was the appropriate penalty for something other than a first offence. And yet the majority of the first offenders in our sample did see their disposition as fair. This suggests that the notion of 'fairness' is more complex than commonly thought. It seems to us that these children were, in fact, expressing feelings of relief at the court's decision not to remove them from their home. Seen in this light, any disposition other than removal from home is 'fair'. The fact that, objectively at least, the circumstances of the offences would in few cases have merited custodial sentences serves to highlight the child's fears of the unknown disposition and his realisation of the extent of the court's power over him. The child is objectively aware of a scale of penalties, but fears that this time the magistrates may deviate from that scale.

In view of the child's appreciation of a tariff it was not surprising to find that the majority of the children thought that the supervision order was made as a result of the nature of the offence they had committed. Only two children pointed to reasons other than the offence as the rationale for the order. ('They said it would help me because my Mum's not around.')

All the children said that they had been told by the magistrates in court to report to their supervising officer at regular intervals. The majority of the children said that the regularity of reporting to their supervisor was the most onerous part of the supervision order. Many described it as 'boring' and 'routine'. ('It's just a chore having to get up and go down there and hang around waiting. Sometimes I've been down there and she's not been there so I've walked out.') Some children made alternative arrangements in order to avoid the regularity of reporting. ('Sometimes I pop in [to the office] to avoid going at regular times.') For most children the main impact of the supervision order lay in the requirement to report to the supervisor, which was seen as a tangible restraint on their liberty to which they had to succumb. ('I have to see her, it's imposed by the law.') Thus, although the relationship which developed between the supervisor and the child was usually described as friendly, this was seen as additional to a more fundamental aspect of the order: the routine of reporting.

A similar picture has emerged from research on residential institutions for delinquent children. Despite the change in name from approved schools to community homes, the children who find themselves in such places clearly see themselves as 'sent away' because of their behaviour. The language of 'welfare' and 'needs' does not hide this. As one boy put it:

> I was told that I was sent here because it would help me, because I wasn't getting on at home at the time nor at school. But I don't believe it. I think it was because I was nicking.

While in material terms the standards of the schools come as a pleasant surprise to children, they realise the limitations on their liberty. Though they may well see what goes on in the institutions as helpful, this is only while they can get something from it – education, a job, or even the lesson that next time things will be worse!

These feelings are not limited to juvenile offenders. To talk of other forms of 'misconduct' in benign language does not mean that what is actually done to or for the child is necessarily in his 'best interests'. The views of clients of the child-care system reveal similar discontent. The National Children's Bureau booklet *Who Cares?* by Page and Clark (tellingly subtitled 'Young People Speak Out') tells us that, despite good intentions, children are acutely aware of the stigma of being 'in care'. They say, for example:

> Being in care you feel you've got a cross on your back. You feel marked (*Who Cares?*, p. 17).
>
> People think that if you're in care you must have done something wrong. The first question they ask is 'What did you do?' It's not just teachers and other kids at school but it's the kids and staff in children's homes. When you go to a new place before you've got your feet in the door they say 'Hey, what are you in for?' (*Who Cares?*, p. 16).

Throughout the book there are vivid illustrations of children's appreciation of the total nature of institutional life and of their resentment of it. In addition, the children frequently express feelings of powerlessness, over both their immediate situation and their future. One child, for example, tells how changes of placement are arranged:

> One day the social worker comes round and says 'O.K. lads, we're going for a ride' and 2½ hours later they end up in another children's home (*Who Cares?*, p. 30).

Another describes case reviews:

> What happens, you see, they talk about you, what you are trying to think. Well, how do they know what you are thinking if you are not there? (*Who Cares?*, p. 42).

Another child speaks of the failure of the institution to equip children to cope with life on leaving the institution:

> For the first time in your life you are making real decisions about yourself, and as you are not used to this, it is truly survival of the fittest. It's easy to see why so many of us get into trouble with society. We can very easily become lost souls (*Who Cares?*, p. 55).

Conclusion

Merely providing more 'resources', developing new institutions, or even putting the principles of treatment into practice will not alter this. Major reviews of research into the effectiveness of penal measures both in the USA and UK provide no ground for optimism. It is not at all clear that doing something is better than doing nothing, or that doing one thing is better than doing another. It is also now clear that intervention can harm as well as help, and that the actions of even the well-meaning do as much harm as good. Awareness of these limitations leads us to seek a radical alternative – justice for children.

4

New Directions: Delinquency and Diversion

There continues to be major debate throughout the United Kingdom about the future direction of juvenile justice policy, but ideological conflict and confusion has marred progress to such an extent that rational argument has become difficult. This chapter aims at rethinking juvenile justice policy and offers a blueprint for the reform of the juvenile court.

Previous chapters have shown that we know little about the specific causes of crime and successful methods of eradicating it. This means that principles of treatment cannot be the primary basis for the juvenile court's jurisdiction. We cannot continue to act on the basis that treatment works or may work some time in the future. Currently treatment does not work. Children also suffer from our continued attempts to subject them to treatment; they require protection from it.

False premises

Because the imposition of coercive measure requires justification, an alternative basis for juvenile justice policy must be sought. Currently there are three broad aims within our penal system: retribution, deterrence (both individual and general) and treatment or reformation. (The protection of society is encompassed within each of these aims.) In any particular case these aims may be entangled: one penal measure may include a number of aims. The fine, for example, has elements of retribution, general deterrence and individual deterrence. There may also be elements of conflict within these aims: reformative aims may conflict with deterrent or retributive aims. In our search for principles to guide future action it is useful to examine each of these aims briefly.

Retribution is punishment in its purest form: it has no other motive than that of inflicting pain for the act done. Retributivists argue that while punishing a man, it is possible to deter others, reform him, protect society and so on, but these are additional benefits, not reasons for punishment. Rather, the offender is given the punishment he deserves. Many people find the notion of retribution distasteful, but it is possible to reject retributive aims and accept retributive assumptions. For example, a retributive penalty would not be conspicuously out of proportion to the crime. To borrow from Biblical language, it would be 'an eye for an eye' and not 'a head for an eye'. The aim of adjusting suffering to sin, of relating the gravity of the offence to the penalty, is not, however, without difficulties. It means assessing the culpability of the offender and the degree of harm ensuing from the offence. Measures are, within this framework, only imposed on the offender for wrong done and not for potential harm. The retributivist is not against reforms but he would argue that these have nothing to do with punishment. Any such arrangements must be optional, for freedom of choice is necessary; otherwise they become part of the punishment.

The remaining penal aims can, collectively, be described as utilitarian: that is, punishment is justified by the value of its consequences. The aim of individual deterrence, for example, is to instil regard for the law through fear of punishment. A major difficulty with both individual and general deterrence, however, is the determination of limits. Is *any* punishment justifiable to deter this offender or potential offenders? Limits of 'compassion' or 'decency' can be imposed, but they are variable and vague. Moreover detection rates for criminal behaviour are often low. In 1977 only 41 per cent of offences known to the police in England and Wales were cleared up. In some cities detection rates are much lower, especially for property offences. This means that only a small proportion of the total amount of crime committed ends in conviction. What effect is this likely to have on potential and actual lawbreakers? There is little systematic research in this area, but a few examples are worth mentioning.

Four hundred American taxpayers were divided by Schwartz into four matched groups: a 'sanction' group (interviewed and reminded of the penalty for tax evasion); a 'conscience' group (interviewed and reminded of their civic sense and feelings of duty); a 'placebo' group (interviewed but not reminded of the penalty or their civic duty); and a fourth group (not interviewed at all). Tax returns were compared for the year before the experiment and the experimental year. The reported gross income in the 'sanction' and 'conscience' groups showed increases; a small decrease was observed in the other two groups. This seems to suggest that attempts to stimulate the fear of a penalty and the conscience do affect behaviour. The project, however, is rather artificial; in the real world offenders are not reminded of penalties immediately before the commission, or contemplation, of an offence.

It seems also that certain offences are more likely to be deterred than others. In 1944, for example, the German forces in Denmark deported the police, which led to an immense increase in the number of robberies and thefts, but to no comparable increase in murder or sex offences. Of course, this indicates that it is *detection* rather than penalties which deters.

Other research suggests that the criminal justice system has, at best, an indirect effect on general socialisation rather than an impact in each 'crime' instance in which pros and cons are weighed in a rational manner. For example, in a British Government Social Survey 43 per cent of those interviewed said that they were constrained from committing offences by their conscience or self-image; 47 per cent were also concerned with being identified as criminals. But the most important consideration was what their *family* would think of them. This research raises questions about the appropriateness of deterrence as a basis for policy deliberations.

Deterrence, however, is rarely seen as the sole justification for punishment; commonly it is combined with treatment or reform. We have already discussed at length the limitations of this approach, and this section no more than summarises the main themes. The underlying notion in reform is to make the offender not only different from what he was, but better. The major difficulty with this is the prevention of excess. Books such as *1984* and *Brave New World* present us with the possibility of a conforming, regimented, benevolent world in which the criminal law, perhaps under another name, is used as an instrument of coercion in the guise of reformatory treatment. Reformation also entails the unjustified infringement of human rights for it is easy to deny legal protection on the ground that the offender is being 'reformed' rather than punished. But 'treatment' often takes place in understaffed, cheerless, firmly disciplined institutions; and certainly it cannot be justified by its results. Unfettered benevolence threatens basic values of human dignity and liberty. Reformation also justifies the application of measures to potential offenders. But predictive techniques are now generally considered unreliable – they over-predict, and thereby subject to our inadequate measures many more children than would otherwise be justified.

Towards change

There are, then, a number of statements we can make which stress the need for a new direction:

1. The criminal and juvenile justice systems are ineffective instruments in correcting, deterring and preventing delinquency.
2. Increased professional services (psychiatric, psychological, social work, etc.) are, generally speaking, not likely to 'reform' the delinquent or, where 'reform' is possible, they are unlikely to be morally acceptable.
3. The earlier a person enters the criminal or juvenile justice system, the more likely he is to commit further offences (through both self and official labelling processes).
4. Harsh penalties are no more effective than mild penalties in reducing recidivism; nor are they more effective as deterrents.

The research data to support any single rationale as a basis for policy are equally unconvincing, and so one is left with determining priorities as much by rejection of alternatives as by empirical investigation. We suggest that *justice* and *fairness* should be key concepts in any new system, and that the juvenile justice system itself should be but a small part of a broader system of responses to criminal behaviour, the aim of which is social education. An overriding concern, supported by empirical data, is the need to minimise the harm likely to accompany coercive intervention.

Preventing crime is, of course, preferable to punishing criminals. But prevention is a complex and comprehensive aim. It depends on identifying and removing many of the difficulties experienced by young people (though not exclusively) in our society, whether they are educational, social, economic or personal, and changes directed at the individual and his family are not sufficient; changes in opportunities for employment, education and recreation must also occur. A comprehensive preventive system must operate at a number of levels: long- and short-term, social as well as individual. Crime-prevention policy (and, therefore, juvenile justice policy) is just one aspect of general social policy. This means that our proposals are necessarily limited; they tinker with the *status quo*. But social change does not lie in our hands. Our proposals are offered as a short-term solution to the deficiencies which currently exist in the juvenile justice system. It is impossible to construct a wholly objection-free system. The task must be stated in another way. How can the principles underlying the juvenile justice system be modified so that we can obtain a *less* objectionable system than we have at present? It is also impossible to construct a pure model where one's intention or hope is to present a scheme which is politically acceptable and likely to be implemented. Compromises are inevitable; we hope to have kept these to a minimum.

Why divert?

Few of us can honestly say that we have never committed a criminal offence, especially as children, but few of us have experienced the sanctions of the criminal justice system; if caught we were dealt with informally by neighbours, parents, schools, employers and so on. The point is that there are a variety of ways in which society can express its disapproval for those who commit wrongful acts. A judicial response is only one method of promoting the social education of the community. Although the commission of wrongful acts may require some kind of response, a judicial response is not, in our view, always necessary or desirable. Because we are in favour of minimum intervention with the lives and liberty of children and of the development of different types of responses to delinquent behaviour, we support the current trend towards keeping children out of the juvenile court, commonly called diversion.

The juvenile court itself was originally planned to divert children from the more formal court procedures applied to adults, and many of the arguments now presented for keeping children out of the juvenile court derive from a feeling that the juvenile court has failed – failed to provide the sort of care envisaged by the proponents of the early courts, and failed either to stem increasing rates of juvenile crime or to reduce recidivism. Diversion is not a soft option. It is founded on the belief that positive and constructive responses to delinquency are possible outside a court forum and that often court appearances exacerbate the very difficulties sought to be resolved. The vast majority of delinquents, especially those not detected, emerge from delinquency into responsible adulthood.

There already exist a number of traditional screening agencies: the community, family, school, social services and police. Children are referred to the juvenile court where these agencies have failed to achieve, or attempt, a resolution of the situation. Stable or rural communities, for example, are more willing to use alternative, informal methods of handling troublesome young people than unstable or urban communities. Similarly middle- or upper-class families possess more numerous and varied resources, both formal (e.g. referral to psychiatrist) and informal (e.g. an offer of compensation), which allow them to find alternative means of controlling their children. Our proposals seek to extend these alternative methods of social control to a wide range of children.

Many minor offenders currently appear in our juvenile courts. In 1977 32 per cent of males under 14 found guilty of indictable offences were given conditional discharges by the juvenile courts; a further 22 per cent were fined. The figures for the 14–17 age group were 20 per cent and 39 per cent respectively. Such dispositions are even more common for those convicted of non-indictable (less serious) offences. The juvenile justice system is too heavy-handed (and expensive) for such offenders; the criminal law and its processes should be a last and limited resort.

The main argument in favour of diversion is that it can prevent the stigma and negative consequences of a court appearance. It has been suggested that the process of arrest, trial and conviction changes the self-image of the juvenile. He increasingly sees himself *as* delinquent, acts *as if* delinquent, and others respond to him as if he *always was* delinquent. There is certainly some evidence for this view; Farrington has shown that court processing intensifies a deviant self-image and leads to further acts of delinquency. Diversion can also avoid contamination: it can prevent naive offenders from meeting the more experienced.

This is not to say that diversion is without its difficulties. Pressure can be placed on children and parents to admit guilt in order to avoid an appearance before the juvenile court. Diversion can mean greater interference with the offender's liberty than if he was dealt with by the juvenile court; it can lead to discriminatory practices (for example, in the exercise of discretion); it can extend, rather than limit, the network of social control; and it can cause increased interference with the liberty of those offenders still dealt with by the juvenile justice system. There are examples of these effects in many current diversion programmes. But they are not essential features of diversion. Discretion, for example, can be structured and limits can be placed on the extent of intervention within a diversion programme.

Who diverts?

A crucial question is who should make the decision to divert a child from the court? We shall consider first the role of the police, who are after all a critical factor in any system of screening and pre-trial diversion. The police in England, as in most jurisdictions, have a discretion not to prosecute. This can be exercised informally on the street, and we can never assess the extent to which this occurs. But the police can also decide to give a formal warning to an offender as an alternative to prosecution. In 1971 just under 83,000 males were cautioned by the police; this had reached over 111,000 by 1977. Almost all of this increase is attributable to an increase in the number of children cautioned. For example, in 1977 13 per cent of detected male offenders in England and Wales were cautioned; 77 per cent of these were juveniles.

Most police areas in England now have juvenile bureaux which decide whether or not to refer particular children to the juvenile courts. Once a child comes to the notice of the police and it is established on the face of it that the child has committed an offence, the police officer in the case submits to the bureau a report setting out the facts of the offence. Bureau staff then collect information about the child from their own records, from the social service department, from the child's school and from any other relevant agencies, and usually visit the child's home. On the basis of this information the chief inspector in the bureau decides which course of action is the most suitable for each particular child – to prosecute, to caution or to take no further action.

The juvenile bureau scheme is intended as a form of diversion: it is based on the principle of keeping child offenders out of court wherever possible. But, although cautioning of males under 17 remained constant between 1971 and 1977, there was a considerable increase in the number found guilty at court. In all, the number of males proceeded against in the juvenile courts in 1977 increased by 18 per cent over the 1971 figures. This could be explained in a number of ways, e.g. by a vast increase in serious juvenile crime, but what evidence there is calls this explanation into question and it is possible to suggest that the existence of juvenile bureaux has led to a widening of the net of social control rather than diversion from it – that is, children who would previously have been dealt with informally are now referred to juvenile bureaux, precisely because such agencies exist, and are subsequently formally cautioned. Juvenile bureaux, for example, have actively encouraged the reporting of offenders by schools, shopkeepers and the like, and so there is a tendency to report to the police many juveniles who previously would have been ignored or dealt with informally.

Concern about the workings of the juvenile justice system has generally concentrated on its formal procedures. Yet often informal procedures like the exercise of police discretion are quantitatively more significant than formal ones, and they are the base-line for further mechanisms of delinquency control. Research indicates that police reactions to offenders depend on such factors as the seriousness of the offence and the age, sex, appearance, demeanour and family status of the offender and that the police, in their 'on the street' decisions, tend to focus on attitude and appearance because they lack other information.

Another concern relates to the variability of cautioning rates. In England, for example, they vary from a low of 27 per cent in Cleveland to a high of 70 per cent in Devon and Cornwall. This may reflect different crime patterns in different areas, but this is by no means clear.

These criticisms of juvenile bureaux in England raise the question whether or not the main role in diversion should be with the police. In this context it is useful to refer to experience elsewhere. Procedures to keep children out of the juvenile court are by now well developed in the USA and Canada. In 1967 the United States President's Commission on Law Enforcement and the Administration of Justice recommended the creation of Youth Service Bureaux in order to remedy some of the defects of the juvenile court. In fact, the

Commission said that the 'formal sanctioning system should be used only as a last resort'. The bureaux are intended for:

1. youths who have not committed criminal acts but whose problems (at home, in the school, etc.) might lead them to do so if they are not helped, i.e. potential delinquents;
2. delinquents whose behaviour is rooted in similar problems.

They are usually located in schools or community centres and are primarily served by the police, who then make use of community resources.

By 1971 it was clear that many agencies with differing and conflicting rationales claimed the label of 'Youth Service Bureau', perhaps in part because of the availability of massive Government funding. Bureaux were something of a growth industry. In 1967 there were only about half a dozen bureaux; by 1971 more than 150 such organisations were in existence throughout the country.

The bureaux are an example of a recurrent difficulty in the practice of diversion. Where such schemes exist, police officers, teachers, and the like seem reluctant to return children directly to their homes for informal handling. This has been called 'the overreach of treatment': children are 'treated' rather than absorbed into the community or tolerated. Indeed, the bureaux are in essence creating secondary probation departments, attached to the police department. Rather than providing an *alternative* to juvenile justice processing, the model has duplicated and further confused the existing system. For example, Duxbury, in an evaluation of the youth service bureaux in California, found that only 12 per cent of all referrals in 1971–2 were from law-enforcement agencies (a further 9 per cent came from probation officers) and these tended, in the main, to be of potential delinquents. This suggests that the bureaux were not operating as *real* alternatives to the juvenile justice system.

A further possibility for diversion from American juvenile courts occurs at what is generally called the *intake* stage. Most intake units are located within the probation department. Originally they were established to screen out cases in which there was insufficient evidence on which to act. A secondary, and now more important, function is to remove from the court's jurisdiction those cases which can be dealt with informally. The case begins with the intake investigation and interview and ends with dismissal, informal handling or referral to the prosecutor. About one-half of all children referred are handled informally by the intake department. The following description shows what this can mean.

The Sacramento County Diversion Programme began in 1970. It dealt firstly with what are commonly called in America 'status' offenders (truants, runaways, etc.) but the project was later expanded to deal with children who had committed petty theft and other minor offences. The programme includes short-term family crisis therapy. The Bronx Neighbourhood Youth Diversion Programme makes use of community residents as mediators in hearings which attempt to resolve disputes between troublesome juveniles and their families (truants, children in moral danger, etc.). It is said, however, not to work well with offenders. Other projects were designed to provide job counselling and placement for older juvenile offenders.

These programmes are not, however, without their critics. To ensure fair and uniform handling it was intended that the decision to divert should be based on *offence* rather than social data. However, a national sample survey of intake procedures found *no* apparent relationship between type of offence and intake decisions; other factors such as family background and school record appeared to play an important role. Indeed, the same survey revealed that routine processing of cases was common and that most juveniles were diverted only from formal court-room hearings to informal handling by probation officers. Furthermore, 45 per cent of the probation officers interviewed reported that they told youths the diversion referral was for a 'trial period' and that if they engaged in further delinquency they would be referred to court and dealt with more severely. Diversion in this context is a sham.

The Canadian approach is similar to the American. In British Columbia, for example, the most common programme or procedure offered to diverted offenders is some form of short-term counselling for the juvenile and his family. This may be supplemented by referral to one or more of a number of social services (e.g. school counselling services or adventure training programmes). Recently there has been an expansion also in the use of restitution and victim or community service. Figures recently produced gave probation officers' caseloads. For those areas available, the picture in June 1976 was as in Table 1. Diversion counselling clearly forms a considerable part of the workload of Canadian probation officers, but the kinds of criticism made of the American procedures are also made of the Canadian.

TABLE 1

	Preventive counselling	*Diversion counselling*	*Probation*	*Other supervision*
Adults	1.6	0.5	93.9	0.9
Juveniles	6.4	18.6	73.8	1.1

In Scotland, a country of broadly similar socio-economic and crime patterns to England, a different mechanism for diversion reduced the number of children appearing before the children's hearings (the Scottish equivalent of the juvenile courts) by 45 per cent between 1970 and 1976. The Scottish system of police cautioning is similar to that in England, although there are no police juvenile bureaux there. About one-fifth of the children referred to the police each year are dealt with in this way. The police then refer those whom they are unwilling to caution to the reporter – the key figure in the Scottish system. It is the reporter's function to decide whether or not the child referred to him is in need of '*compulsory measures of care*' – in other words, whether or not the child can be diverted from the formal social control system. To do so, the reporter gathers information about the child's actions, school behaviour, social characteristics and family background, and pieces this information together. The significance of the original ground of referral – for example, theft – is understood by the reporter by considering the action in its wider social context. The decision taken depends on the type of picture which emerges.

The reporter begins with the report of the referring agency (which, in the majority of cases, is a report from the police) giving details of the offence or offences which are the reason for the referral. But it is clear from the fairly high proportion who are not referred to a children's hearing that the original ground of referral, particularly in offence referrals, is not necessarily seen in itself as indicating a need for compulsory measures of care. The reporter attempts to distinguish between the 'normal' delinquent and the 'problematic' delinquent, between the 'normal' runaway and the 'problematic' runaway. Only when the reporter believes that compulsory action is necessary is the child referred to a hearing. Built in to the Scottish system, therefore, is a *double* screening device. The reporter stands as an independent and visible sift between the police and the children's hearings. This has meant that many of the cases actually referred to the reporters by the police are not subsequently referred by them to the children's hearings: 49 per cent in 1976.

Reporters were created as a professional group only in 1970. What kind of people are they? The Kilbrandon Committee – the Committee whose recommendations led to the new Scottish system – felt that the role called for 'a degree of practical knowledge and understanding of children's problems' and that a reporter 'should preferably be an officer combining a legal qualification with a period of administrative experience relating to the child welfare and educational services'. Such creatures are rare to find, and, in fact, the majority of the reporters appointed in 1970 were lawyers or social workers. (Other groups were also represented – for example, former police officers and clergymen.) By 1977 the majority of reporters were social workers.

What happens to these children? No action by the reporter can include an interview or letter in which the reporter warns the child of the consequences of his action, voluntary social work or psychiatric help for the child, restitution, compensation, community service and so on. The limits of action lie in the imagination of the reporter and the consent of the child. Our favourite anecdote concerns two boys involved in fire-raising. This was dealt with by sending the boys along to the local fire-station, where they were shown round by the fire-master as he discussed with the boys the dangers of fire. This response to childish misbehaviour is, to our mind, far more constructive than any traditional measure which could have been imposed by the juvenile court. But, in many cases, it does also mean that nothing formal happens to the child – an acknowledgement that delinquency has many meanings and requires a variety of responses.

Perhaps not surprisingly the police have been the main critics of the new system in Scotland. They feel that, in some cases at least, the best interests of the child are not served by taking 'no action' and that the most criminally minded children will regard 'no action' as an inducement to commit more crime and to continue on a criminal career.

Indeed, the police are unlikely to become an integral part of a diversionary approach towards children in trouble – such values have a low or marginal position in the values of their profession. The central duties of the police are the prevention, control, and detection of crime, and the normal end product is to take the individual to court. To ask the police to be the main agency for keeping children out of court creates a conflict in the various roles to be performed by an individual officer, and leads to conflict with his colleagues.

It is for this reason that we feel there is a strong case for an *independent* sifting mechanism between the police and the juvenile court. The reporter system in Scotland provides an example of the kind of framework we have in mind. It seems to us preferable to those frameworks already developed in Canada and the USA, where a group of professionals previously part of the juvenile justice system merely extended its role. Such an approach runs the risk that those charged with diversion will be influenced by prior role orientations and by the demands and expectations of fellow professionals. This is less likely to happen where a new profession with specific functions is created.

This is not to say that the reporter system is perfect. It operates within a supposed treatment system and so is influenced by these criteria. In addition, although the reporter alone is responsible for the decision to refer the child to the hearing, there is no machinery for appeal against his decision; there are no criteria set out anywhere for determining whether or not compulsory measures of care are necessary; the decision is made in private; and the reporter need not give reasons for his decision.

The operation of the Scottish system also alerts us to a further danger in diversionary schemes. Though reporters referred fewer children to the hearings than had previously been referred to the juvenile courts, once the children reached the hearings, the level of intervention was greater than that in the juvenile courts – more children were placed under the supervision of social workers and more were removed from their parents' homes in 1976 than in 1970. (In 1970 3,529 children were placed on probation by the juvenile courts; in 1976 4,133 reports to the hearings were made subject of supervision requirements, an increase of 17 per cent. In 1970 1,208 children were made the subjects of approved school or fit person orders; in 1976 1,752 children were removed from their homes by the hearings and, in addition, a further 229 were removed by the courts, an increase of 64 per cent.)

This greater level of intervention highlights a deficiency in a model of non-intervention. It suggests that referral to a court should be a measure of last resort – a sign that all else had been tried and failed. This assumes that the court will know better how to deal with those appearing before them, but there is no reason to suppose that this is so; for, if all else has been tried, what can courts do other than punish these children? This means that children are controlled and punished often in the guise of 'care' or 'treatment'. Such children also continue to be stigmatised perhaps to an even greater extent than in other kinds of system because they are, by definition, the *most* troublesome, the *most* disruptive and so on. For this reason discretion in the juvenile court must be restricted.

The practice of diversion

None of these deficiencies are inherent in diversion. Acceptance of the principle of non-intervention requires the establishment of sifting mechanisms to ensure that only those in need of compulsory intervention enter the juvenile court. Sifts can operate in both a mandatory and a discretionary context. We propose that first- and second-time offenders who commit minor offences should be automatically cautioned by the police. ('Minor offences' in our scheme would mean class 1 offences. We explain what we mean by this on p. 71.)

Research exists to support this suggestion. In Wolfgang, Figlio and Sellin's 'birth cohort' study (which followed through a sample of boys from birth to 18) it was found that 46 per cent desisted from crime after the first offence; of the remainder, 35 per cent desisted after the second and approximately 25 per cent at each remaining step after the third offence. They called this process 'spontaneous desistance' and argued that intervention should be held in abeyance until the commission of the third offence. Individual responses at an earlier stage are wasteful, as most children cease their delinquency regardless of further action. It could, of course, be argued that these children were deterred by their court appearance. But this must be weighed against research which suggests that official labelling in court *increases* the likelihood of the child committing further acts of delinquency. Negative consequences can flow simply from the child's referral to the formal justice process.

The juveniles diverted by the police would be formally warned by them of the consequences of continued delinquent behaviour. Thereafter the police would have to consider the appropriateness of diversion carefully in each case and present reasons for the decision to refer the child further into the system. It would be possible to structure police discretion further than we have proposed, but we have decided against this. Current practice indicates that the nature of the offence, previous record and age are already the main criteria in the decision whether or not to caution. The fact, however, that the police would have to present reasons for their decision to refer the child on does provide some constraint on abuse. In all these cases the admission of guilt by the child *per se* would not be sufficient grounds for action. The case against the child would have to be supported by confirmatory evidence. Legal advice would be available to the child if he so wished. The current safeguards which exist with respect to interviews of children by the police would continue. Social service, educational and other specialist help would be available to any child, but it would be for *the child* to accept or reject such help.

Where the police decide against warning the child (or where there is a dispute as to the child's guilt), they would refer the child to an independent sift, who would again ask the question whether or not the offence was sufficient to warrant compulsory intervention by means of a court order. There are likely to be differences of opinion on the criteria which should be referred to in this decision, but we present the following as a starting point for discussion:

1. the seriousness of the alleged offence(s);
2. the circumstances in which the offence was allegedly committed;
3. the previous offence history of the child;
4. the existence of alternative social, educational, legal or other measures;
5. any plans put forward by or on behalf of the juvenile to make amends;
6. the civil remedies available to the victim;
7. the extent to which public rights or interests are affected.

The articulation of specific criteria limits arbitrariness in the administration of the law and protects, to some extent, the rights of the young people in question. Certain criteria should be statutorily excluded: for example, the social and family characteristics of the child.

If the case does not need formal intervention, the sift could decide that no action need be taken, or that some informal action be taken. This decision, we feel, should be jointly reached between the sift, the child (after legal advice), and perhaps the victim. A relevant factor in the process must be the child's willingness to accept alternative social and legal measures. This is frequently rejected by commentators on the ground that the child may feel some pressure on him to agree to informal action in order to avoid formal referral to the juvenile court. A requirement that the child should consult a lawyer before accepting any such proposals meets this objection. The child's response to previous informal 'action' is also commonly rejected because failure may be the fault of a particular diversion programme as much as of the child. But we feel that this is also a relevant factor in the decision whether or not to take (further) informal action. We view diversion as a series of 'responses' rather than 'programmes' and, to this extent, this objection loses much of its validity. To do otherwise denies the child's responsibility for his own actions and future. If the child does not accept the sift's proposal, the sift may refer him to the court if action is thought to be necessary. A further criticism made of diversion is that it can frequently mean greater intervention with the life and liberty of the child than formal referral to the juvenile court. To meet this we propose that the maximum length of time in which the informal action (for example, community service) could operate would be one-third of that possible within the juvenile court. (Custodial sanctions would not be available at all. Sanctions within the juvenile court are discussed in the following chapter.) There would, however, be no enforcement procedures. If an agreement breaks down, this is a relevant piece of information in any subsequent proceeding.

Reasons would be given for the decision to refer the child to the juvenile court, and the decision could be challenged in the juvenile court before the case was heard. Similarly, where the child disputes his guilt, he would be referred to the juvenile court if the sift felt that further action was necessary. At this stage also the prosecutor would review the case to establish that *prima facie* grounds for referral existed.

Conclusion

There are, of course, dangers in this emphasis on diversion. It may become just another tunnel that the child enters and then emerges for the next stage in the process. Old ideas may become recycled (many current schemes repeat the inadequacies of similar programmes previously offered by the courts) and processing can become routinised – the child is allowed an additional bite at the cherry, that's all. Indeed, it has also been suggested that emphasis on diversion runs the risk of taking attention away from more fundamental issues and basic reforms – that it is a further example of society's over-reaction to the normal problems of adolescence. There is some truth in this. It is for this reason that we argue for increased tolerance within society for minor offenders: strong reactions exacerbate the long-term problem for society. It is also for this reason that we stress that juvenile justice systems do not and cannot affect crime rates. To achieve this, wider social changes, through the medium of social, income and economic policies, are necessary.

Diversion is a framework worthy of further consideration: the full weight (and expense) of the juvenile justice system is too heavy-handed for the bulk of juvenile delinquency. In general our proposals seek to develop new structures or procedures whereby offenders can be dealt with in a humane and fair way without recourse to court proceedings. Our intention is:

1. to persuade the community, family and school to respond informally to lawbreaking;
2. to emphasise positive and constructive responses to delinquency (e.g. reparation by the offender to the victim or to the community);
3. to engage, where possible, the victim directly in working out a settlement (either informally through the parents or formally through the independent sift);
4. to emphasise the responsibility of the offender (in a way in which we feel formal processing often ignores);
5. to provide the offender with guidance, supervision and other assistance in coping with any difficulties *he* may feel he has.

We seek to prevent what is becoming a dominant trend in juvenile and criminal justice policy: the transferring of the problems and responsibilities of the family, school and community into the public domain.

5

New Directions: Justice in the Juvenile Court

Dissatisfaction with the operation of the current juvenile court could take us in a number of directions. Some researchers in England have already called for the abolition of the juvenile court. Priestley, for example, has suggested that children who are suffering from parental neglect or abuse should be dealt with in family courts and that the age of criminal responsibility should be raised to 15 or 16. Children below this age who commit offences, he argues, should be dealt with in the main informally or by a formal police caution. But if the offences of such a child constitute a serious threat to the safety or well-being of other people, then a new kind of public protection proceeding, to be heard in the Crown Court, is recommended. The aim of such proceedings would be to secure the detention of the child, not necessarily in his own interests, but in the interest of the public. A protective custody order would commit the child to secure accommodation for a definite period, and could be appealed against or reviewed at 3-monthly intervals.

While we agree with much of this, there are problems. First, it is not politically or popularly acceptable for the age of criminal responsibility to be as high as 16. Children know the difference between right and wrong at a very young age and, although the current age of criminal responsibility (10) was arbitrarily chosen, it represents the age at which it is generally felt that legal accountability can be imposed. If Priestley means that children who commit offences under the age of 16 would be dealt with by civil proceedings, he offers no solution: the confusion which currently confronts the operation of the juvenile court would remain. In addition, it is likely that many children would become subject to public protection proceedings in the Crown Court, an experience from which we protect most adult offenders. Moreover 'serious threat to the safety or well-being of other people' is left undefined, and is open to the same subjective stereotyping which has currently created the so-called 'hard-core' of juvenile delinquents.

Another proposal (by the British Association of Social Workers) is that the Children and Young Persons Act 1969 should be fully implemented. The Scottish system of juvenile justice provides a case study of what this would look like in practice. There, high levels of intervention in the lives of children and their families occurred through the re-emergence of the principle of the offence as the primary criterion of intervention supplemented and reinforced by a subjective and stereotypical image of the delinquent. Although 'treatment' was the *official* goal priority, control of the child's behaviour became the *operational* goal priority. Research suggests that the hearings, in fact, operate on tariff principles just as in the juvenile courts. Initial decisions by the hearings are founded on a modified tariff of deeds supplemented by reference to the child's social characteristics (i.e. his needs). This, in turn, is translated into a tariff of dispositions in which discharge precedes community-based supervision and community-based intervention precedes removal from home. The fact that over half the children in List D schools (former approved schools) in one research project had previous supervision experience and that few had no previous court or hearing experience at all provides some support for this claim. Further evidence for the existence of tariff considerations comes from Bruce and Spencer's work, which shows that panel members themselves are acutely aware of the need to protect the public and often give precedence to this obligation over consideration of the needs of the child. What is promoted, therefore, as a welfare jurisdiction is no more than the replication of the practice south of the border.

The childrens' hearing system in Scotland demonstrates the effect of some of the theoretical criticisms we have already made and suggests that the answer to the current difficulties in the juvenile court does not lie in full implementation of the 1969 Act. We feel that the juvenile court (and the current age of criminal responsibility) should be retained but that the court's role should become that of administering justice in the traditional meaning of that term: intervention on the proof of commission of the offence and proportionality of sanction to offence. It is essential that the mechanics of the decision-making process and dispositions meet parents' and children's expectations. Where this does not occur, the clients may withdraw their support from the court and, with it, their legitimation of the social control process. The juvenile court should only deal with those children whose behaviour is so persistently or seriously delinquent that they cannot be dealt with by diversion. It should be concerned primarily with safeguarding society's safety and reinforcing community norms rather than with the 'needs' of children. It should not be concerned with 'treatment' but rather with ensuring that the rights of the child are adequately safeguarded and with determining the appropriate disposition for the offence. It would also adjudicate on the issue of guilt in cases where the offence is denied.

Certain principles are now set out to meet this shift in the orientation of the juvenile court.

The principle of the commission of an offence

Commentary

Traditionally the juvenile court has had jurisdiction over children's non-criminal misbehaviour: truancy, moral danger, running away from home and so on. This jurisdiction should be removed from the juvenile court. The judicial system is an inept instrument for resolving family or school disputes. Such children should be dealt with by a system of voluntary referral to services in the community. Compulsory intervention should be restricted to certain limited emergency situations; this jurisdiction should lie within the proposed family court.

Practice

The jurisdiction of the juvenile court would be limited to those offences which are punishable when committed by an adult.

The principle of proportionality of sanctions

Commentary

Disposition patterns reveal widely different approaches in the use of particular sentences from one court to the next, which can lead to a sense of injustice among the young people appearing in those courts. Accordingly we propose that sanctions for juvenile offenders should be proportionate to the seriousness of the offence(s) which they have committed. This requires two things: a classification of offences and a classification of sanctions.

The difficulties inherent in developing an index of seriousness of offences are well documented, but they are not irresolvable. Some classifications are rather crude. One American report, for example, proposes five different categories (and, therefore, sanctions) within burglary. It looks like this:

1. When committed while the lawful occupants were at home and when the defendant brandishes a weapon in their presence: 24 months' imprisonment.
2. When committed while the lawful occupants were at home but under circumstances in which the defendant, although armed with a weapon, did not confront them or brandish a weapon in their presence: 18 months' imprisonment.
3. When committed in an unoccupied dwelling by a defendant armed with a weapon: 12 months' imprisonment.
4. When committed in an unoccupied dwelling by an unarmed defendant: 6 months' imprisonment.
5. When committed in a clearly abandoned dwelling: probation for 6 months.

A similar scheme was proposed for other offences: six categories of homicide, three of aggravated assault, three of rape and so on. These categories, because they are descriptive and isolate only some of the essentials of the offence, could be more or less numerous: there could as justifiably be five or seven categories of homicide as six.

A similar though simpler scheme, specifically in relation to juveniles, has recently been proposed by the American Bar Association. It recommends that there should be five classes of juvenile offence, determined by the maximum sentences authorised on conviction of an adult offender. For example, a class 1 juvenile offence is any offence which would be punishable by death or imprisonment for life or for a term in excess of 20 years where committed by an adult. Likewise, a class 5 juvenile offence is any offence which would be punishable by imprisonment for a term of 6 months or less were it committed by an adult. The Bar Association also recommends three types of sanctions. From the most to the least severe they are:

(a) custodial (confinement in a secure facility or placement in a non-secure facility);
(b) conditional (e.g. restitution or periodic reporting to a probation officer);
(c) nominal (e.g. warning).

The maximum duration of the sanction is determined by the class of the juvenile offence. The maximum penalty for a class 1 offence is 24 months' confinement in a secure facility, and for a class 5 offence it is 2 months' placement in a non-secure facility, provided the child has a prior record; otherwise the maximum is a conditional penalty for 6 months.

Alternatively, more sophisticated schemes could be adopted. Wolfgang, for example, has proposed a scale based on the seriousness of the social harm inflicted by the offender on the community. By assigning offence scores to each offender, he obtained cumulative scores for offenders over time. Many minor offences then add up to the same score as a single major offence in the child's record. It is thereby possible to indicate the level of social harm created by the child, and Wolfgang has suggested that this could be linked to society's response to the child. The child would know what point he had reached in the scale of penalties and what form future responses would take. Such a scheme, according to Wolfgang, would provide a rational basis for establishing sanctions with more consistency than now exists and might well increase the deterrent impact of sanctions.

In these different proposals there are different methods not only of fixing the seriousness of the offence, but also of determining the sanctions. In the first American report referred to the appropriate sanction for each offence was fixed. Judges could look, however, to aggravating and mitigating factors which refer, generally, to the issue of culpability. In the American Bar Association proposal the judge has a limited choice between the three types of sanction but has considerable discretion within these sanctions, both to the length of time the child would be subject to the sanction and to the choice of the particular programme. The standards recommend that once the category and duration of the disposition have been determined, the choice of the particular programme should be governed by the needs and desires of the child.

Practice

Each of these schemes has advantages and disadvantages. We have derived from them what we feel is practicable within a British context. We propose six categories of offences and three of sanctions.

In English law there already exists a broad classification between summary and indictable offences. The latter are, generally, the more serious. We have called summary offences class 1 offences, which include drunkenness, disorderly behaviour, vagrancy and offences involving pedal cycles. Indictable offences cover a wide range of seriousness.* Some indication of the level of seriousness of a particular offence is given in the maximum penalty for that offence. (We are not arguing that this is necessarily the best indicator; it is, however, readily available.) Recently the Advisory Council on the Penal System prepared a review of maximum penalties, and proposed dramatic reductions. For example, the current maximum penalty for burglary is 14 years' imprisonment; the Council proposed a new maximum of 3 years. Similarly the current maximum penalty for blackmail is 14 years' imprisonment; the Council proposed a new maximum of 5 years. The principle on which these new maximum penalties was reached was determined by reference to the sentence length below which 90 per cent of all sentences of immediate

* There are offences which are triable in the adult criminal courts either on indictment or summarily. These offences, known as offences triable either way, would be dealt with in our scheme as if they were summary offences unless the prosecution established the case for dealing with them as if they were indictable offences (for example, the powers of the juvenile court in relation to summary offences have been exhausted or are inadequate in light of the nature and circumstances of the offence). No rules govern current prosecution discretion but practice in the juvenile court should be consistent with that in the adult courts, where the vast majority of offences are dealt with on a summary basis.

imprisonment imposed on offenders convicted in the Crown Court fell: 96 per cent of burglars are sentenced to less than 3 years; 94 per cent of blackmailers are sentenced to less than 5 years.

We banded together those offences with similar maximum penalties and created five further classes of juvenile offences. The following presents some examples:

Class 2 offence (where the proposed new maximum is 3 years): assault, theft, deception, criminal damage, assault occasioning actual bodily harm, handling, possession of drugs and indecent assault.
Class 3 offence (where the proposed new maximum is 4 or 5 years): forgery, affray, possession of firearms, burglary, blackmail, grievous bodily harm, wounding and arson.
Class 4 offence (where the proposed new maximum is 5 years): robbery and aggravated burglary.
Class 5 offence (where the proposed new maximum is 7 years): buggery and rape.
Class 6 offence (where the proposed maximum is life imprisonment): manslaughter and murder.

We propose that there should be a tripartite division of sanctions: nominal, custodial and non-custodial. Table 2 sets out the proposed limits to the powers of the juvenile court.

TABLE 2

Offence	*Non-custodial*	*Custodial*
Class 1	3 months	1 month
Class 2	6 months	3 months
Class 3	12 months	9 months
Class 4	18 months	12 months
Class 5*	not applicable	not applicable
Class 6*	not applicable	not applicable

*These offences can only be dealt with in the Crown Court and we discuss those dispositions later.

We have set an upper limit of 12 months for custodial sanctions and of 18 months for non-custodial sanctions. Whether or not the particular maxima proposed adequately meet the conflicting demands of justice (proportionality and determinacy) and the protection of society is a matter for discussion. But a fundamental assumption in our argument is that some such limits ought to be prescribed. The limits proposed have been derived from an awareness of the adverse effects of long-term institutionalisation, scepticism about the ability of sanctions to prevent the repetition of delinquent behaviour, and an examination of the current disposition practices of the juvenile court.

The custodial sanctions currently available to the juvenile court are detention centre orders (in practice 6 weeks), care orders (in practice 12 months in a residential institution) and borstal training orders (the current average period of detention is 9 months). Our proposed custodial maxima reflect current *practice*. The indeterminate nature of some of the current custodial sanctions conceals differences in the seriousness of different offences. For example, the average period of detention for theft is 9 months, for burglary is 9 months and for robbery is 9 months. (This estimate was reached by adding together, in weeks, all periods of detention imposed on juvenile offenders for these offences and by dividing this by the number of offenders given these dispositions.) Yet only 10 per cent of male thieves, 21 per cent of male burglars and 36 per cent of male robbers sentenced in 1977 were given custodial dispositions. This presumably reflects the seriousness with which such offences are viewed by magistrates (who in turn, arguably, reflect public opinion). Our proposed maxima have taken this factor into account. Offences of different seriousness should be *seen* to be different.

Proposals on these lines mean that penalties imposed in the juvenile court would differ markedly from those imposed on adults in the criminal justice system. A 17-year-old could receive a long term of imprisonment for behaviour which subjects those under 17 to a much shorter term of detention. There is 'injustice' in dealing with two offenders who commit like acts so differently merely as a result of age. But our proposals for juveniles could serve as a model for the criminal justice system. This falls outside the scope of this book, but it is worth noting that penalties for adult offenders in some European countries are far lower than those currently imposed in this country. In Sweden, for example, only 10 per cent of offenders are given prison sentences and only 10 per cent of those receive sentences of more than one year. Two-thirds of all receptions into prison are for less than 4 months. In the Netherlands short prison sentences are even more marked: less than 3 months is the norm. The limits of non-custodial penalties also seek to make proportional the limits of intervention to the offence, but the maxima proposed are of longer duration than for custodial sanctions so that they may be viewed by sentencers as realistic alternatives to custodial sanctions.

Where a child has committed more than one offence during the same episode, we suggest that the juvenile court should not be able to impose a sanction more severe than the maximum sanction authorised for the most serious of these offences. Sanctions, on the other hand, could be combined (e.g. a custodial sanction followed by a non-custodial sanction), provided the total duration of the sanction did not exceed the maximum term of the custodial sanction permissible for the offence.

Unlike a strict proportionality model of justice, our scheme takes into account previous offences. This is not, as some have suggested, because persistence makes the current offence somehow more 'serious'. Rather, it is because it accords with *clients*' views of the juvenile justice system: children expect something 'more' to happen to them if they offend again. Moreover children see it as unfair if co-accused are dealt with in the same way as them when co-accused have committed more (or less) offences. But the effect of a previous record would differ markedly from the current situation; it would not provide the opportunity for *disproportionate* incursion into the child's life.

We propose that where a child is found guilty in the juvenile court of an offence on four occasions within 6 months the court *may* impose a sanction which would have been possible had the offence been of the next most serious class. (By 'occasion' we include separate proceedings arising out of the same transaction; stealing a car while absconding from a custodial institution and committing burglary on the way would be one occasion although it might involve a series of proceedings.) Similarly we propose that where a child is found guilty in the juvenile court of an offence on eight occasions within 12 months, the court *may* deal with it as if the offence was two classes more serious. (These suggested limits are open to debate. We have deliberately set them high to mark the seriousness of the step taken.) The court would be required to state the reasons for such dispositions in writing. The only exception to this would be that, where the number of previous appearances would increase the class of offence so that it fell within the jurisdiction of the Crown Court, magistrates would not be allowed to assume that power: they could either sentence the child within their powers or refer the case to the Crown Court.

The Crown Court, as presently constituted, would deal with juvenile offenders in two situations: children charged with class 5 and 6 offences where a judicial response was thought necessary (there were 34 such defendants in 1977) and those cases referred to the Crown Court by magistrates where they felt that their powers were inadequate to deal with the offender.

The powers available to the Crown Court in respect of classes 5 and 6 offences would be the same as those of the juvenile court but with upper limits of 3 years' and 5 years' custody respectively. While these proposed maxima are open to debate, the Advisory Council on the Penal System recently recommended that the maximum penalty for buggery and rape should be reduced from life to 7 years for adult offenders. With respect to murder and manslaughter, the existing maximum penalty is life imprisonment, but the current average period of imprisonment for life sentences is 10 years. Our proposals are not out of line with these recommendations, given the youth of our subjects.

In those cases referred to the Crown Court because juvenile court magistrates felt their powers of disposition to be inadequate, there would initially be a pre-disposition hearing to determine the merit of the magistrate's referral (i.e. to determine whether or not the sanctions available to the juvenile court had been made full use of). The Crown Court judge at the disposition hearing would have all those powers available to the juvenile court, but, where it is established that the juvenile court's powers are inadequate, he may sentence the juvenile to a maximum of 2 years' custody.

The principle of determinate sentences

Commentary

Since we have rejected principles of treatment in favour of concepts of justice and fairness, our proposed sanctions refer only to *past* illegal behaviour and reject any reference to predictions of future offences. We also reject individualised and indeterminate dispositions which give substantial discretion to both the judiciary and the executive to decide how to meet a child's 'needs' and whether or not (and when) these 'needs' have been met. Current practices in the juvenile court have resulted in arbitrary decision-making. Cultural biases, subjective attitudes and sexual discrimination have all been shown to be part of official discretion, so that wide disparities in sanctions imposed for the same offences have resulted.

Social enquiry reports, though retained, would have a fundamentally different role and character. These reports are traditionally based on opinion rather than on scientifically based fact, and their current use is premised on the mistaken belief that we know what the 'needs' of a particular child are and what the appropriate disposition to meet those 'needs' is. We do not know, and we should not pretend otherwise.

Practice

The nature and duration of the disposition would be determined by the court at the time of sentence on the basis of the offence. The nature (i.e. seriousness) of the offence would determine the limits of the sanction: the circumstances of the offence (for example, the nature of the child's involvement) would determine the choice of sanction within that limit. Social enquiry reports would be factual check-lists of the child's age, record and present offence. It should also contain a statement of the child's willingness or otherwise to participate in certain disposition alternatives.

The disposition imposed by the juvenile court could not be subsequently modified. Children would not be discharged from institutional placements, for example, as a reward for conformity. Appeal against dispositions would, however, continue to be available to both parents and children.

The principle of least restrictive alternative

Commentary

There is little evidence that known 'treatments' for delinquency have any rehabilitative (or deterrent) effect. Reconviction rates are high and there is some indication that intervention may hinder employment prospects and lead to further delinquency. Consequently we propose minimum intervention with the lives of young people.

Practice

Within the sentencing bands set out the juvenile court must choose the least restrictive category and duration of disposition which is appropriate to the seriousness of the offence, as modified by the degree of the offender's culpability and by his prior record. There would be a presumption against custodial dispositions and against placement in a secure facility. Only the Crown Court would have the power to impose a period of secure custody. The imposition of a particular disposition would be accompanied by a statement of the facts relied upon by the magistrates and the reasons for selecting a particular disposition and for rejecting less restrictive alternatives. This statement would form the basis of any challenge to the disposition (where, for example, it does not adequately reflect the nature and circumstances of the offence or where there appears to be a gross disparity with general sentencing practices).

The principle of the juvenile's right to counsel

Commentary

Although the number of lawyers appearing in the juvenile court has increased in recent years, legal representation is not common. Moreover the current role of the lawyer in the juvenile court is confused, depending more on whether or not the court sees itself as a forum for justice or welfare. (This is discussed in Chapter 7.)

A juvenile justice system which is fully acknowledged to be adversarial and to be responding to what children *do* rather than to what they *are* makes clear what a lawyer's duty is: first, to test the legal sufficiency of the case against the child and, second, to prevent or minimise court action. In the former he would act as now before an adult criminal court (e.g. he would cross-examine witnesses and introduce evidence on behalf of the child). At the disposition stage he would argue for intervention which is proportional to the offence and is of the least restrictive type.

Practice

We propose the right to counsel for all children in delinquency proceedings and at all stages in the proceedings, and that the child should be entitled to legal aid. The most convenient method by which to ensure this would be an extension of the duty solicitor schemes which currently operate in some courts.

The question has arisen in some jurisdictions as to whether or not this right to counsel should be waivable. In our view a child should be able to waive his rights to counsel. This is in line with the need to stress the child's responsibility for his own actions. It would, however, be open for the child subsequently to challenge any sanction imposed on him while unrepresented if it could be shown that he did not fully appreciate the nature and consequences of his action.

The principle of limitations on intervention prior to adjudication and disposition

Commentary

In 1977 some 8,000 children were remanded to the care of the local authorities and some 4,000 were remanded to prison facilities prior to a finding of guilt or sentence. Of the former some 50 per cent were ultimately not received into care and of the latter 37 per cent did not receive a custodial disposition. This suggests that the current juvenile justice system is increasingly willing to intervene in the lives of children where the 'trouble' they have been said to cause has not been proved or where it has not subsequently merited a custodial response. This practice continues despite the fact that prison as a disposition for children under 17 was abolished in 1908.

Concern over the remand of children in prison facilities has recently led to the introduction of criteria to make such remands less frequently used. But it remains to be seen whether or not they will have this effect. Even if fewer children are remanded in prisons, the social services network continues to expand in order to house children who are remanded in custody. While this may be a more humane form of containment, it remains containment.

Practice

In a system in which a custodial response to juvenile delinquency is a last resort, there should be an affirmative duty on decision-makers to release juveniles before adjudication or disposition and to justify, in writing, any decision not to do so. We propose that, on the arrest of a child, the arresting officer should (1) inform the juvenile of his rights, including the right to silence, and (2) notify the child's parents and/or the child's lawyer (where the child requests one) of his arrest. On arrest we recommend that the juvenile *must* be released if the offence for which he has been apprehended is a class 1 offence. In all other classes of offence the arresting officer *may* release the child. This discretion should be exercised in the juvenile's favour, but where a child is detained, he should be brought before a magistrate within 24 hours.

Where apprehended children have been so detained, magistrates would be required to release the child pending the hearing unless:

1. The child has committed an offence, the nature and circumstances of which indicate the likelihood of serious injury to others if the child were to be released.
2. There are grounds to believe that the defendant
   (a) has a recent record of failure to appear at juvenile courts proceedings; or
   (b) is likely to interfere with witnesses or otherwise obstruct the court of justice.
3. The child having been released on bail, has broken a condition of bail.
4. The child has requested custody for his own protection.

Where custody is shown to be essential, there would be a presumption in favour of placement in a *non-secure* facility (e.g. remand hostels, remand foster parents, etc.). Where a secure placement is made, a written statement of the reasons for this decision must be provided, and the decision may be appealed against. Any period spent in custody pending the hearing of an appeal would be deducted from any disposition subsequently imposed as a result of that hearing.

The principle of visibility and accountability of decision-making

Commentary

We have already drawn attention to the subjective nature of much of the information used by the juvenile courts in the decision-making process. Our aim is to limit this discretion and to recommend the development of guidelines for decisions at each stage of the proceedings.

Practice

Accordingly, formal criteria for referral to the juvenile court should be set out for each of the decision-making stages, so far as is practicable. We made some suggestions with respect to this in the previous chapter. Reasons for decisions would also be stated in writing – for example, where a child has not been diverted from the court process and why a particular disposition was chosen. Similarly, where magistrates wish to refer the case to the Crown Court on the grounds that their powers are inadequate, a written statement of the reasons must be produced. Appeals from the decisions of the magistrates would be to a Crown Court judge in chambers. Appeals from the Crown Court against conviction and sentence should follow the present format for adult cases. The powers of the Queen's Bench Division to hear a 'case stated' on a point of law or to review the case by means of prohibition or *certiorari* should remain.

Postscript on penalties

The aim of sanctions imposed by the juvenile court is to indicate the unacceptability of the child's behaviour and to impose some constraint on the child. The sorts of sentence we have in mind are conditional, deferred or suspended sentences; fines, restitution and compensation; community service and community supervision. With respect to custodial penalties this could be both intermittent (night, week-end, or weekly custody) or continuous. Our proposals seek both to limit the courts' powers in relation to the duration of an order and to provide flexibility in the use of orders.

Dispositions form a tariff of penalties ranging from least to most incursive. Within each class of offence the whole range of tariff options should apply. Many of the penalties we have outlined are already available to the juvenile court; but, in so far as the system proposed is primarily concerned with controlling or penalising delinquent behaviour, the nature of these penalties is radically altered.

Supervision, for example, becomes a method of controlling the offender within the community. The question for the sentencer who is considering a supervision order is not 'Does this offender need help?' but rather 'How much control does this offender deserve in light of the nature and circumstances of the offence he has committed?' Consequently supervision periods could be of much shorter duration (e.g. 1 month, 3 months, etc.). We do not mean to prevent the supervisor providing, and the offender accepting, a variety of 'helping strategies'; but these must be extraneous to the formal requirements of the disposition. Breach of the order would only occur where the formal requirements of the order as set down by the court were not met. Rejection of 'helping strategies' would not amount to a breach and could not be commented upon in any subsequent court appearance by the child. The new form of supervision order would permit a helping relationship to develop; it would not mandate it.

Community service orders provide another flexible mechanism by which the juvenile court may respond to children who offend. By combining elements of restitution and penalty, this order is well suited as a response to a variety of juvenile misconduct. In keeping with the need to develop proportionate penalties, we envisage the development of a tariff of hours of community work which would relate to other sentences in the juvenile justice calendar. Pease has provided one illustration of what community service could look like in such a system. He suggests that orders up to 100 hours should be imposed only in cases in which the order is not viewed by the magistrates as an alternative to custody and that orders of 240 hours (the current statutory maximum) should be regarded as equivalent to a custodial sentence of not less than one year. Other penalties (fines, supervision, etc.) could be related to custodial penalties in a similar way.

With the rejection of principles of treatment, institutional placement also takes on a new role: restraining the liberty of the child. By abandoning notions of 'diagnosis' and 'treatment', we abolish existing distinctions between institutions for observation and assessment and those for long-term care. Allocation on the basis of the child's 'needs' would be expressly excluded. This means that institutional placements for delinquent children would no longer be limited to the inaccessible locations of the existing community homes with education on the premises. In fact we recommend that these institutions no longer be used for children. Rather, the plethora of observation and assessment units which have developed within local centres of population should be used as institutions to serve the custodial needs of the local community. By locating these resources within the child's community, we can minimise the disruption to his personal life (e.g. to his family ties, educational links, etc.) and reduce the conditions in which breakdown of institutional placements have been shown to occur. We propose that the use of facilities for delinquents outside a local authority's geographical boundary should be prohibited.

Within these newly designated facilities it is unlikely that daily life would look very different from that which occurs currently. Our intention is to promote a homelike (rather than institutional) environment in which a small number of children (e.g. a maximum of 20 per unit) of both sexes are cared for by qualified residential staff. In rejecting rehabilitation as an appropriate goal for the juvenile justice system we are *not* rejecting the goal of offering help to delinquents. As with supervision orders, 'helping strategies' may be offered to children, but children should not be compelled to accept so-called therapeutic services. Implicit in this principle of optional treatment is the belief that while the justification for intervention is the offence, the child *himself* may recognise the need for some services. Participation, however, must be voluntary. This recognises the child's right to decide on actions affecting his life and freedom. As far as possible community-based facilities should be made use of rather than creating special facilities (e.g. schoolrooms) within the institution. Children would not be penalised for refusing to continue to participate in any counselling, treatment or training programme. We believe that helping services (such as education) must be made relevant to children. If their relevance is perceived, children will use them.

Part II
Care and Justice

6
The Legal Basis of Care

On 31 March 1977 over 100,000 children were in the care of local authorities in England and Wales. Of these, nearly 81,000 were in care because of the inability of their parents or guardians to provide for them. About half (46,600 children) stay in care for only a short time. The average stay is less than 8 weeks, although about a quarter stay in care for up to one year. Reception into care for the majority of these children is a response to an emergency within the family: hospitalisation, desertion, or homelessness.

The rest of the children stay in care for much longer periods. Currently 42 per cent of them stay in care for between 1 to 3 years, and a further 52 per cent remain for over 3 years. More than half of these children come into care under the age of 10, and in 1977 a third of the receptions were under the age of 5. The local authority acts as the parents of these children.

The routes through which children find themselves in care are diverse. The grounds on which local authorities can assume the position of parents or guardians have continually been expanded during the twentieth century, and existing legislation provides a maze through which it is difficult to travel. Two features, however, dominate the legal status of children received into care. First, the criteria for intervention are vaguely defined. The need to show that the child is in 'moral danger', that his 'proper development is being avoidably prevented or neglected' or is 'beyond control' and directions that decision-makers should act in 'the best interests of the child' establish a wide ambit of discretionary power within the various courts dealing with children. Secondly, children – the subjects of the proceedings – are, in fact, the objects. Existing legal arrangements are primarily designed to facilitate a contest between the natural parents and the state over the custodial rights to children. The structural arrangements by which these rights are determined reinforce the marginal position of the child: for example, the child is entitled to legal representation but his views may not be presented. But parents, too, are in a marginal, or at least disadvantaged, position through the unequal distribution of legal rights and the practical difficulties which exist in securing independent professional services to aid their case. Subsequent chapters elaborate these points, and some are discussed in Chapter 3. This chapter outlines the main legal provisions for receiving children into care.

In voluntary care

Under section 1 of the Children Act 1948 local authorities have a duty to receive into care children whose parents (or guardians) for various reasons are unable to care for them. The route into care for such children is informal and non-judicial – that is, it is by agreement with the parents (or guardians). The route out of care should be equally informal, as local authorities have power to exercise control over children only for so long as the parents agree. If a local authority wishes to exercise permanent legal control over a child voluntarily in its care, it must obtain a resolution, from the elected members of the local-authority council, that it can assume full parental rights and duties. If parents object within 28 days of receiving notice of this resolution, the matter is referred to the juvenile court for adjudication.

Section 1 broadly defines the categories of children whom the local authority has a duty to receive into care: children who are orphaned or abandoned and have no one to care for them; and children whose parents or guardians are prevented by some incapacity from providing for their upbringing. A child is received into care on these grounds only where 'the intervention of the local authority is necessary in the interests of the welfare of the child'.

Since section 1 only specifies a duty to *receive* and not to *take* a child into care, the placement in care is essentially voluntary. Parents do not relinquish their rights, although they do lose the day-to-day control of the child while he is in care. It seemed that local authorities had to return the child to the parents or guardian on their request (although this was not always done), but this was amended in the

1975 Children Act, so that, once a child has been in care for 6 months or more, the parents or guardians must give 28 days' notice to the local authority of their intention to remove the child from care. If the local authority wishes to assume full parental rights and duties over the child, certain criteria and procedures have to be met. It is normal practice for the social services department of the local authority to present a resolution to the council asking for parental rights to be vested in the council. The criteria for assuming full parental rights and duties are set out in section 2 of the 1948 Children Act. These require some element of parental unfitness or inability to care for the child properly, abandonment of the child, or the death of the parents. The 1975 Children Act, partly as a response to the death of Maria Colwell and partly because of research into the consequences for children of being left in care for a long time, added two further grounds. The first allows a child to be made the subject of a resolution when only one parent is unfit; the second allows local authorities to pass resolutions where the child has been in voluntary care for 3 years *without* the need to prove parental unfitness (in order to facilitate the adoption of the child).

Once a resolution has been passed by the local authority, the parents must, unless their whereabouts are unknown, receive written notice of it and be informed that they have 28 days to object in writing. If the parents object, the local authority must refer the matter to the juvenile court within 14 days; otherwise the resolution lapses. In these proceedings a local authority seeks to obtain from the juvenile court confirmation that full parental rights in respect of a child already in voluntary care should be vested in the local authority. The court has to be satisfied of three matters before it can uphold the resolution: that, at the time the resolution was passed, there were grounds for making the resolution; that those grounds still exist; and that it is in the child's 'best interest' to confirm the resolution. The parents may at any time apply for a discharge of a resolution, in which case the juvenile court only considers whether or not it is in the child's interests to discharge the resolution. (Where parents seek to establish that there was no ground for making the resolution, the application must be made within 6 months.) The 1975 Children Act enables either the local authority, parents or guardians to appeal to the Family Division of the High Court against any confirmation or revocation of a resolution.

Proceedings, whether in the Family Division of the High Court or in the juvenile court, are between the local authority and the parents (who can apply for legal aid). The child is neither present nor participates in the proceedings. A clause in the Children Act 1975 which empowers the court to join the child as a party and appoint a 'guardian *ad litem*' in order to safeguard the child's interests is not yet in force.

Involuntary care

The criteria for taking children into care compulsorily are set out in the Children and Young Persons Act 1969. These proceedings encompass two main categories of children; first, the abused and neglected and, secondly, the troublesome. The grounds which have to be proved before an order vesting parental rights in the local authority can be made are laid out in section 1(2) of the Act. Technically, the proceedings require three steps:

1. Proof of one of the primary conditions (for example, the child is neglected or in moral danger).
2. Proof of the secondary condition that the child is in *need of care or control.*

If one or other is not proved, then the case must be dismissed. But if the court is satisfied that both the primary and secondary conditions are proved, the juvenile court can go on to

3. The disposition decision.

Before examining the practice of care proceedings, we must describe briefly interim orders. Place of safety orders authorise the removal of a child from an unsatisfactory environment for up 28 days and his placement in a place of safety, usually a hospital, a children's home or foster home. The obtaining of such an order is a simple and quick procedure. It does not require the detailed presentation of evidence before the juvenile court, nor do the parents have to be notified that an application is being made. Indeed, neither the parents nor the child can take part in or oppose such an application. Anyone acting in the interests of the child can apply to the juvenile bench during court hours or to a Justice of the Peace out of court hours. The magistrates have to be shown by the applicant that:

1. he has reasonable cause to believe one of the conditions specified in the Act exists; or that
2. a juvenile court will probably find that the child will be ill-treated as this has already happened to another child who is or was a member of the household.

In practice, the applicants for a place of safety order are the local authority or the NSPCC. Once the order has been issued, the child can be removed to a place of safety. The police can be called to assist if there is any opposition to the child's removal, and, indeed, the police themselves possess wide powers authorising them to remove a child to a place of safety (for up to 8 days) for the same reasons (except truancy) without the need first to obtain the permission of a juvenile court or magistrate.

A place of safety order grants to the local authority the power to make decisions about the child's day-to-day care. There is no appeal against the granting of such an order, but the parents or any other interested person can attempt to make the child a ward of the High Court and seek the discharge of the place of safety order in wardship proceedings.

Before the expiry of the place of safety order, the local authority must decide whether or not to initiate care proceedings or allow the order to lapse. (The police and NSPCC can also be applicants in such proceedings.) Place of safety orders are not renewable beyond a period of 28 days. To allow an order to lapse and then to re-apply would be an abuse of the court process. If the local authority wishes to retain care of the child, care proceedings must be begun before the expiry of the order. Usually, in the first instance, an interim (that is, temporary) care order is sought by the local authority.

The juvenile court deals with fewer civil than criminal matters, and both have to compete for dates in courts' lists, which are often already full. In the Inner London area, for example, adjournments for hearing dates sometimes extend over a period of up to 6 months. This means that interim care orders are frequently sought and granted. They vest in the local authority full responsibility in matters relating to the child's day-to-day care. Interim orders are granted for a maximum period of 28 days at a time. In some parts of the country, particularly Inner London, difficulty in obtaining a hearing date can mean that a child may be subject to several successive interim care orders and may, therefore, remain in care for several months before the case is finally determined.

The child (unless under 5 years of age) and his parents should be present in the juvenile court for all applications at which an interim care order is sought, and can oppose it. This can be a distressing process. Young children, especially, find the court a bewildering and frightening place. For their parents to be so near and yet so far obviously increases the uncertainty. Children who are unclear about the meaning of the proceedings and who find themselves in a court building containing police, young offenders and probation officers must sometimes wonder if they are there to be punished.

The local authority must present evidence in support of an application for an interim care order, but there is no consensus about the kind of evidence or standard of proof required. In some juvenile courts, the evidence of one key witness or information in a medical report about the child's medical condition will be sufficient; elsewhere the proceedings come close to a full hearing of all the issues.

If granted, an interim care order may be challenged by way of an application for its discharge to a Judge in Chambers in the Queen's Bench Division of the High Court. If this is refused, the High Court's consent and directions must subsequently be sought should the local authority wish to exercise its discretion to allow the child to return to the care of his parents or guardian. Interim care orders are, however, rarely challenged in the High Court.

When the case is finally brought to the juvenile court, proceedings under the 1969 Act, unlike proceedings under the 1948 Act, are between the local authority (or the NSPCC or the police), which is the applicant, and the child, who is the respondent. The amount of participation permitted to the parents is open to some doubt. Unlike the child and the local authority, the parents are not a party to the proceedings and strictly speaking do not have any right to participate fully. (The consequences of the parents' limited right to participation is discussed in Chapter 7.)

The parents do not have the right to appoint their child's lawyer. Similarly the child's lawyer in promoting the child's interests has no obligation to put forward the parents' views. If the applicant's case is proved, further evidence, social enquiry and other reports, may be presented in order to assist or influence the court at the dispositional stage. (Neither the child nor parents have the right to read these.) At this stage rules of evidence are relaxed, but, since it has become common practice to canvas issues which are relevant to the dispositional stage at the adjudicatory stage, social enquiry reports often do little more than provide a resumé of the local authority's case. Juvenile court magistrates are not obliged to make an immediate decision; they can adjourn the case or make an interim care order so that a further assessment of the child can be made or other information obtained.

The juvenile court has two main disposition powers: a care order and a supervision order. A care order grants to the local authority in whose area the child habitually resides all parental powers and duties, although the parents can be ordered to contribute towards the maintenance of the child. The order can continue until the child reaches the age of 18 – or 19, if the child was 16 or over when the care order was made – and, during that time, the local authority may place him in any setting thought suitable to promote his welfare (e.g. a children's or foster home). A supervision order places the child under the supervision of a local-authority social worker (or probation officer if the child is over 13) for up to a maximum period of 3 years, but, in any event, not beyond the child's 18th birthday. The order may contain certain conditions: for example, it may require the child to reside with a named individual or to be medically examined. A supervision order does not give the supervisor the right to enter the home or to remove the child physically. A supervisor who for some reason is unable to perform his duties can apply to the juvenile court for an order requesting that the supervision order be discharged or varied into a care order.

The child (or parent on his behalf*) can apply for a discharge or variation of the order made. Applications must be made at an interval of at least 3 months from the initial court adjudication, and thereafter at intervals of at least 3 months. The supervisor under a supervision order or the local authority named in the care order have a right to make similar applications.

The child (or parents on his behalf*) can also appeal against both the finding of the alleged condition proved and the disposition

* The exceptions to the parent acting on behalf of the child are as follows: where a solicitor is already acting for the child, where the child objects, where the child is alleged to be beyond parental control, and where the court feels there is a conflict between the parent and the child.

decision. On appeal a re-hearing takes place. In spite of the welfare ethos of care proceedings, appeals lie not to the Family Division of the High Court but to the Crown Court, which is primarily concerned with criminal matters.

If, in unopposed applications for the discharge of an order, the juvenile court feels that there is a conflict between the parents and the child, it *may* order that the parents should not be treated as acting for the child. It may also grant legal aid to the parents if it feels that their interests should be protected. If an order for separate representation is made, a 'guardian *ad litem*' may be appointed to protect the child's interests. Although the 1975 Children Act extends this provision to *all* applications in care proceedings, economic stringency means that currently it only affects unopposed proceedings to discharge the order.

The 'guardian *ad litem*'s' duties include making an independent investigation and assessment of the proceedings, considering whether or not it is in the child's interest for the application to continue and, finally, appointing a lawyer or conducting the proceedings himself on the child's behalf. The 'guardian *ad litem*' may also prepare a written report for consideration at the dispositional stage of the proceedings. There is no statutory guidance as to who should perform the role of 'guardian *ad litem*', and so, in practice, the probation service or a social worker from outside the local authority concerned with the child perform this role.

Parents can very easily be excluded from the hearing of care proceedings. They may initially oppose the proceedings, appeal or apply for discharge of the order on behalf of the child, but the child's lawyer may decide to concede the local authority's application. The parents have no *locus standi* with which to insist how the case should proceed, because, in theory, they are not parties to the proceedings.

Children and the High Court

The wardship jurisdiction of the High Court has been invoked by local authorities and parents in order to supplement some of the deficiencies of care proceedings and, in a few exceptional circumstances, to review the misuse of local-authority discretion over children in care. If a child is made a ward of Court, parental rights and powers vest in the Court and the child's day-to-day care is delegated to a named individual who becomes the agent of the Court. This relationship continues until the child's majority or prior termination of the wardship. The Court is responsible for such matters as education, religion and marriage of a ward, and is kept informed of the ward's progress.

Anyone with an interest in the child may instigate proceedings. In one case, for example, an educational psychologist invoked wardship proceedings to prevent the sterilisation of a minor. The minor himself may invoke proceedings through an adult who acts as his best friend, and in such instances the Official Solicitor may be invited to represent the minor. If the Official Solicitor represents the child, the minor is joined as a party to the proceedings. Where the proceedings concern a local authority, the parents have a right to participate as full parties, unlike in care proceedings under the Children and Young Persons Act 1969, and are entitled to legal aid. In this case the Official Solicitor may be invited to represent the minor's interests independently. The minor becomes a party to the proceedings.

The process for commencing wardship is extremely simple and quick. As soon as a summons seeking to make the minor a ward is lodged with the Registry, the child becomes a ward of Court for 21 days. But wardship lapses unless a hearing is arranged with the Registrar within this time. At the first hearing the Registrar gives directions as to how the matter should proceed and refers the case for hearing before a Judge.

The Registrar may order that the Official Solicitor be invited to represent the child or that a welfare officer's report be prepared. Any preliminary points which are in issue and are complex are referred for adjudication by the Judge. The Registrar may order that these matters are dealt with speedily so that the case can receive an early hearing by the Judge.

The protection of the High Court is available to any minor. In cases of extreme urgency temporary orders or injunctions can be obtained before the issue of a summons, if the applicant undertakes to issue the summons later. Where the child's welfare is in imminent danger, an order may be obtained on an *ex parte* basis (that is, without notice to the other side) from any Judge of the High Court at any time.

Where the Official Solicitor has been appointed to act as 'guardian *ad litem*' to the child, his role is to ensure separate and independent representation of the ward's interests. He is an officer of the Court and solicitor to the ward. Although he acts as guardian to the ward, he is a legal officer. The Official Solicitor acts on invitation and cannot himself instigate proceedings. His responsibilities go beyond conduct of the proceedings. He makes an independent investigation of the case with a view to preparing a report for the Court. In so doing, he may interview the ward and other interested persons, instruct medical or other (including social work) experts and instruct counsel to represent the child's interests in Court. The Official Solicitor is not bound to accept the views of the ward or of any expert whom he has instructed; neither is the Court bound to adopt the views of the Official Solicitor.

Evidence is on affidavits (sworn statements), which are exchanged in advance of the hearing so that all parties can be appraised of the issues, but the Court will also require oral evidence from whoever is proposing to have care of the ward. The hearing is more akin to an inquiry than is usual in legal proceedings, in that the judge takes an active part and the rules regulating the admissibility of evidence may be relaxed. Where hearsay evidence is the best available, it will not necessarily be excluded. The judge may interview the ward and parents if he wishes, and proceedings are heard in chambers (in private), although the court may publicise aspects of the case where this is in the child's interests.

The High Court may in *exceptional* circumstances commit a child to the care of a local authority. Unlike the juvenile court, the High Court can make orders outside the provisions of the Children and Young Persons Act 1969. For example, it can make the child the subject of a care order where the statutory grounds are not established. The welfare of the child is the determining factor. Thus, local authorities sometimes invoke wardship proceedings to obtain a care or supervision order on evidence which is speculative rather than positive. This is not common practice, however, as proceedings are expensive (around £1,000).

The High Court can make mandatory or prohibitive injunctions to protect a ward's welfare, and has power to enforce its orders by contempt proceedings. Interim orders may include supervision by the local authority, or access by a parent to a child in care; any matter can be referred back to the Court for further directions or assistance at any time. Where a child is committed to the care of a local authority, the court may subsequently review the matter if it wishes.

Local authorities have no right to appeal against an unsuccessful application for a care order. They can, however, seek an order in wardship proceedings at any time. Parents (who are not parties and who, therefore, have no right of review in care proceedings) have no such right of appeal to the High Court through wardship proceedings. They may, however, be able to invoke wardship proceedings in *exceptional* circumstances. In one recent case parents successfully obtained the revocation of a care order made in the juvenile court. The parents, who were Pakistani, applied to have the child made a ward of Court and sought permission to take the child out of the country to their native Pakistan, where they were returning to live. The Court of Appeal felt that here there were exceptional circumstances justifying the use of wardship.

Sometimes parents, foster parents or other interested persons wish to question a local authority's exercise of its discretion and powers over children in care, or to challenge the decision of a local authority. In *exceptional* circumstances wardship jurisdiction may be successfully used to achieve this. Although any child who is in care may become a ward of Court, the Court is slow to substitute its discretion for that of a local authority. For example, in circumstances in which a child is in voluntary care the Court will only exercise its jurisdiction where it would not interfere with the local authority's discretion. Generally wardship proceedings are not possible at all where the child is in care under section 2 of the 1948 Act. There are, however, a few exceptions to this principle. The Court is prepared to interfere if a local authority is shown to be acting unlawfully, in breach of its statutory duties or in bad faith. In such cases the Court makes a preliminary investigation to determine whether or not grounds for intervention exist.

Where a child has been committed to care under section 1 of the Children and Young Persons Act 1969, the Court will again only exercise its jurisdiction in exceptional circumstances. This has the effect of leaving the natural parents without any means of challenging a local authority's decision to, for example, place the child a long way away from the parents' home, to deny access to the child or to refuse to disclose where the child is living. Local authorities, on the other hand, are encouraged by the High Court to seek its assistance where, for example, they are disatisfied with the decision of a juvenile court.

7
Legal Rights and the Courts

Treatment and justice are not always compatible with one another, but care proceedings attempt a compromise between the two. The requirements of justice can inhibit the imposition of treatment techniques and children tend to have few legal rights in courts with a welfare orientation. Indeed, in the logic of welfare protectionism legal rights are unnecessary. The question frequently raised is 'What does the child need to be protected from?' More recently there has been growing interest in the rights of children, including their legal rights. Certainly the extent of legal representation of children has increased in recent years, but little consideration has been given to the role which the child's lawyer should play. Should the lawyer represent the child or his parents, or both? Should he independently assess the child's interests or follow the wishes of the parents? Should he act as an advocate for the child or as an officer of the court? These are difficult questions in themselves, but they beg a more important question. What do we want to achieve? Should we protect the child's legal rights or try to promote his welfare? Should the lawyer try to get the child off or get appropriate treatment for him? Should he sacrifice the child's legal rights if the child's general welfare seems to require it? Should he look to the child's legal rights and his welfare? This chapter looks critically at the current provision of legal representation and legal rights in those areas in which the state intervenes with the lives and liberties of children and their families.

Children in danger?

Place of safety orders are intended for emergency use only. Their purpose is to remove to a place of safety a child who is in *actual* danger. Such orders, however, are very easy to obtain (it is extremely rare for an application to be turned down), and so there is considerable potential for their abuse and misuse.

It is certainly the experience of many of our social work colleagues that exposition of the grounds to justify such an application frequently takes no more than a few minutes. Sometimes magistrates cross-examine an applicant; others, however, are reluctant to challenge the views of professionals and grant the orders without question. This procedure does not require legal certainty and places a low priority on legal rights. Evidence, although on oath, can be unsubstantiated, opinionated, exaggerated and inaccurate. It is certainly not open to challenge as parents may not know of the application and, where they do, they have no right of representation. There is no right of appeal against a place of safety order; the child can be removed for up to 28 days and, during that time, the parents can be denied all access to their child.

This laxity in the procedure to obtain place of safety orders encourages decisions which are against a child's interests. The removal of a child from its home can cause trauma, distress and long-term harm. Research shows, for example, that continuity of relationships, surroundings and environment is essential to the proper development of a child. Disruptions in the care of a child have varying impacts, according to the age of the child. Separation of a young child from his mother can cause considerable stress and anxiety and can have long-term damaging effects where the substitute care is inadequate.

Yet there has been a considerable increase in the number of place of safety orders (especially since the death of Maria Colwell). In March 1973, some months before the report on Maria Colwell's death was published, there were approximately 214 place of safety orders in existence each week. By March 1977 this figure had more than trebled to 759.

Lawyers experienced in this field can quote numerous cases in which local-authority social workers have over-reacted to unsubstantiated fears. In one case the local authority removed a 3-day-old baby from its mother in hospital because it felt that the child was likely to be neglected. The local authority's application for a full care order, on the same grounds, was later rejected by the court, since the local authority had no evidence to support the grounds.

In another case the speech of a boy of 3 was not developing properly. His mother, who was a single parent, had promised to take him to the clinic on several occasions for diagnosis of his speech deficiency, but had failed to do so. When a further appointment was missed, the social services department removed the child on a place of safety order and placed him in a residential nursery. Care proceedings were then started. There were several interim care orders, which prevented the child's return home, although the mother maintained regular contact with her son. At the full hearing 3 months later the case was adjourned for a further 3 months, owing to lack of time to hear all the evidence. The magistrates refused the local authority's request for a further interim care order and so the boy was able to go home. During these 3 months the child thrived. Yet, at the resumption of the hearing, the social services department still wanted a care order, though they agreed that the child could be allowed to remain at home. The reason given was that they wanted greater *control* in case something went wrong or future appointments were missed. The magistrates did not find the case proved and dismissed it.

This case illustrates two points. First, the social workers were quick to apply for a place of safety order. The child was not in any immediate physical danger and their action could have seriously affected the child's relationship with his mother. Secondly, the local authority requested a care order although it was its intention to allow the child home. This shows the extent to which social workers seek power over families. If parents do not conform to the demands of the social services department, they run the risk of their child being taken away without any further hearing of the merits of the decision.

Place of safety orders clearly deny both the child's and parents' rights, especially where there are no further proceedings or where subsequent proceedings show that the case is not proved. It is clear that many place of safety orders do not result in full care orders. According to the figures for 1977, there were approximately three times as many place of safety orders as there were care orders made under the civil jurisdiction of the juvenile court. But, even where it can be shown that the social services department has acted in error, there is no redress for the parents for the distress and damage caused to them and the child by this removal. While speedy proceedings are essential in order to protect children from danger, disregard of the need for uniform standards and for rigorous judicial scrutiny of the evidence means that many unnecessary applications for place of safety orders are requested and granted.

Inquisitorial or accusatorial?

The Children and Young Persons Act 1969 fails to define the procedure for hearing care proceedings, and so recourse has to be made to the ordinary rules governing civil proceedings in magistrates' courts and to additional special rules applicable in juvenile courts. But these provide no clear guiding principles for the operation of care proceedings in the juvenile courts. This means that there is a lack of consistency in juvenile courts, a fact which has led the Select Committee on Violence in the Family to state that there is a need for certainty and uniformity in care and related proceedings. In addition, parents (and the child's lawyer) have no right to obtain in advance details of the case which they have to meet. This puts them at an immediate disadvantage.

Disputes between parents or relatives over the custody of children are usually decided, on the other hand, by a Judge of the High or County Court. (Some of these cases can be determined in the magistrates' courts but this is becoming less and less common.) In both the High and County Courts, rules of evidence and procedures are clear and well defined. Parties, for example, exchange written information in advance about matters which will be raised at the hearing.

Although decisions taken in both custody suits and care proceedings may be critical to the future of the child, issues in care proceedings are probably of greater significance than those in custody disputes. Whereas custody suits are usually concerned with the readjustment of rights *within* the family, care proceedings go further and challenge the family's right to autonomy and freedom from state interference.

A summary hearing (that is one which is swift, brief and dispenses with formalities and details) is the traditional mode of adjudication in the juvenile courts. Care proceedings are essentially adversarial – a contest between opposing sides played in accordance with specific rules which regulate the mode and type of evidence on which a decision can be made. Since care proceedings are civil, they are governed by civil laws of evidence as well as by special rules of procedure. The evidence before the court must be accurate and reliable; hearsay evidence is generally inadmissible. Each side presents evidence, which is challenged by cross-examination. The picture is one of confrontation and accusation. Procedural tactics and skill in advocacy may prove crucial to the outcome of the case. Magistrates must restrict their decision to the evidence they have heard and cannot themselves call for further evidence, even on the views of the child. Their decision can only be based on evidence which has been presented to them. For example, in the court proceedings discharging the care order on Maria Colwell the court did not hear the views of Maria or of her long-standing foster parents (who, like Maria, were opposed to her returning home). The court was also not informed of Maria's stepfather's violent criminal record, nor was it given any opportunity of meeting or making any assessment of him.

Inquisitorial proceedings, on the other hand, present a contrasting picture. Rules regulating the admissibility of evidence have little relevance and are liberally construed. The court as inquirer has a right to demand and obtain whatever evidence it deems necessary. Recently Lord Widgery (the Lord Chief Justice) suggested that care proceedings should be heard on such a basis. He described them as 'essentially non-adversary, non party . . . an objective examination of the position of the child . . . it is not set up in such a form as to provoke a contest between the local authority and the parents or, even more, the child and parents. It is an objective enquiry . . .' (*Humberside County Council* v. *DPR* (an infant) [1977] 3 AER 964 at 966). A brief examination of the facts of this case explains why the Lord Chief Justice departed from the usual view that care proceedings are adversarial.

The case concerned a young child who had lived with his mother and her co-habitee. The local authority's evidence to the Court consisted of the medical certificates of two doctors as to the injuries to the child and two photographs showing these injuries. The local authority also wished to present witnesses (the police, the NSPCC and others) who would give evidence of incriminating statements which the co-habitee had made to them. The *child's solicitor* objected that, in accordance with the civil rules of evidence, this evidence was inadmissible as it consisted of out of court statements by someone who was not a party and, therefore, was hearsay. The co-habitee had not been asked to give evidence, could not be cross-examined and could not be compelled to incriminate himself. The solicitor wanted the case to be conducted strictly in accordance with the rules and to capitalise on the fact. Faced with this, Lord Widgery relaxed the hearsay rules and avoided the adversarial nature of the proceedings. He said:

> I think that when you have proceedings of this kind, which are *non-party*, then confessions are to be admitted. In other words all that is necessary to be shown is that the evidence tendered is direct evidence of an admission by someone who has control of the child (at p. 967).

The desire to include such admissions is understandable; however, the end result is that parents suffer the worst of both worlds. They are not accorded full party status in the proceedings, and so can only play a limited role; yet they cannot claim the advantages of non-party status – for example, the inadmissibility of their out of court statements. This case establishes a dangerous precedent and conflicts with more widely held views that care proceedings are essentially adversarial. While the informality of round-table forums and the relaxation of procedural safeguards may appear desirable in matters which concern the child's welfare, the issues in care proceedings strike at the root of civil liberties and family rights and so require a legal forum. This does not, however, solve the question of who are the 'adversaries' in the case. In theory the 'adversaries' in care proceedings are the local authority and the child, but in practice, although legal aid is nominally given to the child, the parents handle it, so as, in the words of Lord Widgery, to 'represent the anti-authority view'. This means, in effect, that the local authority and the parents are the 'adversaries' (though the parents are at a considerable disadvantage).

This does not mean that adversarial proceedings are without their difficulties. Magistrates' decisions often depend primarily on their assessment of the family. Notions such as 'obtaining a job', 'the stability of the family' and 'acceptance of voluntary treatment' are, therefore, commonly used by lawyers to *manipulate* juvenile courts in this decision-making process. In a sense the welfare orientation of the court is used by the lawyer *against* the court. Indeed, many lawyers raise the same arguments over and over again (irrespective of the child's or family's situation) because they seem to work! The case of Wayne Brewer, who was returned home after the discharge of a care order and was subsequently killed by his stepfather, illustrates this point. Wayne's lawyer (who identified his client's interests with those of the *parents*) advised the parents to make domestic improvements to their house and to borrow library books on child care. He also advised the stepfather to remain in employment to indicate stability. The lawyer conveyed the impression that the parents had matured and improved since the child was first assaulted by his stepfather. Although the stepfather allegedly had an unpredictable temper, neither parent was cross-examined by the council's solicitor and the stepfather's statement 'I have not got a bad temper' was unchallenged. The tactics of, and selective presentation of evidence by, Wayne's lawyer persuaded the court to revoke the care order and to return him to his family.

The court's welfare orientation can, of course, also work against the lawyer. There is some American research which suggests that such courts have resisted attempts by lawyers to introduce elements of justice or due process. Consequently lawyers were prevented from acting *as lawyers*. Certainly the role (and, therefore, the value) of the lawyer is bound up with the role of the juvenile court and the way in which it responds to particular cases.

Juvenile courts seem to adopt one of two distinct approaches – justice or social welfare. The 'effectiveness' of legal representation, therefore, cannot be assessed by uniform criteria; what is 'effective' representation in one judicial setting may not be in another. Indeed, it is likely to be extremely difficult to impose an adversarial system on courts which view themselves primarily as agencies of social welfare. It may be difficult to convince a welfare-orientated court that the child's best interests are secondary to the requirement that one of the conditions of the Act must first be proved. Research suggests that magistrates and social workers in a welfare-orientated court consider that lawyers have little understanding of its philosophy and role.

The child's lawyer?

The Brewer case illustrates another fundamental inadequacy: the lack of separate legal representation for parents and children. Currently the child and not the parents is eligible for legal aid (except in unopposed discharge proceedings), which means that the lawyer for the child may feel that he should act as if for the parents. Indeed, as the child's legal aid is assessed on the parents' income, parents may have to make a financial contribution to it. Although they cannot actually choose the lawyer, parents may, nevertheless, expect the lawyer to accept instructions *from them.* This is obviously fraught with difficulties, but where the lawyer does act for the child to the exclusion of the parents, this can mean that only part of the picture is presented to the court. These ambiguities mean that the interests of the child, parents and justice are in jeopardy.

Until recently little attention was paid to the need for separate representation of children from their parents in care proceedings, and to the particular position of the parents in these proceedings. Rules introduced in November 1976 did, however, enable parents to meet *allegations* raised in the course of proceedings. But this is no panacea, especially while legal aid is still denied to the parents. The very question of what is, or is not, an allegation against the parents is open to some doubt. Indeed, arguably, merely to *bring* care proceedings alleges that the parent is failing to provide the requisite care for his child. It is difficult to imagine any greater need for independent legal representation than that of parents whose parental rights and responsibilities are threatened. Invariably in care proceedings parents stand or feel accused, particularly where the issue is child abuse or neglect. Yet independent legal representation remains the exception rather than the rule. This means that information (which may be subjective, out-of-date, etc.) remains unchallenged and continues to form the basis for intervention with the family. It seems fundamentally unfair for the state to seek the removal of a child from a parent without giving the parent the right to legally aided counsel. Currently there is an imbalance between the parties. Separate legal representation to both child and parents is common practice in many American states: for example, New York.

Furthermore, since parents are not a party to or respondent in the proceedings in the juvenile court, they have no right of appeal against the court's decision. This right lies solely with the child or with his advocate. If neither exercises this right, the parents are virtually powerless. It is easy to see how the process of care proceedings can prove baffling to parents, especially if they have had no legal advice and if their child is too young to give his opinion. The advocate for the child can disregard the parents' instructions and can, if he wishes, concede the local authority's case.

Although legal aid is more frequently granted to children in care proceedings now than previously, it is doubtful that their interests are protected or promoted. Presenting children's interests depends upon the attitude, integrity and ability of the advocates (many of whom are young and inexperienced) assigned to represent them. In some instances the child may be too young or immature to instruct his lawyer, who then has to apply his own judgement on issues of both a legal and non-legal nature. Matters of a social, medical and psychiatric nature are not part of a legal training.

This means that the lawyer frequently does no more than add *his* weight to the social enquiry report or repeat its favourable aspects. On occasions, however, where the social worker recommends removing the child from his home, the lawyer may oppose this by offering information not contained in the report as a basis for argument, or he may suggest that the report has glossed over the special circumstances of the case. This, it has been suggested, can lead to tension or conflict with others in the court, such as social workers, who consider that the lawyer is being disruptive.

Current procedures mean that the child's advocate has competing and conflicting demands made on him by *all those* participating in the proceedings. His role can be either that of an adversary to the local authority, adversary to or advocate for the parents, or a quasi 'guardian *ad litem*' to the child. Alternatively, he can act as a friend of the court and adopt a legalistic but neutral stance, advising the court on law and fact. This ambivalence results in part from the restricted degree of participation allowed to the parents, but also from recent attempts to impose an inquisitorial approach over the traditional adversarial approach in care proceedings.

While cases like those of Wayne Brewer and Maria Colwell are clear examples of the failure to ascertain or independently promote the child's view or position, another dilemma arises in circumstances in which the child gives instructions which, in the lawyer's assessment, are wrong or could jeopardise his well-being. In one case, the parents of an 11-year-old schoolboy refused to send him to a comprehensive school. Care proceedings were brought and a care order was made. The matter was taken through various appeal courts and the Court of Appeal finally confirmed the care order. The Court, however, criticised the way in which the child's case had been conducted. The boy's lawyer promoted the father's objections to comprehensive education and called him as a witness on behalf of the child. As the lawyer felt that the father's views complemented the child's case, he did not challenge these views. However, in the Court of Appeal, Lord Justice Cumming-Bruce expressed some concern. What troubled him was the fact that the child's interests might not have been the same as the father's. He said:

> I have a haunting fear that the fact that the interests of the child may have been confused with the interests of the father may have made it difficult for the court . . . to appreciate what the child's interests were. It may be that in cases raising issues as the present, the legal advisers of the child should consider very carefully how far it is consistent with their duty to the child to present a case which appears to be identical with that of a parent who holds somewhat obsessive views (*Re DJMS* (a minor) [1977] 3 AER 582 at 591).

The evidence in the particular case, however, suggested that the child did share the father's views. The Court's reasoning seems to imply that the child's lawyer had some duty to ignore his client's views in circumstances in which they were in conflict with established notions of the welfare or interests of a child. This interpretation is untenable: the lawyer's role must be to advise the child and zealously pursue what he requests of him. Where a child is old enough to advance his views, the mere fact of his youth is no justification for denying him representation of those views through a lawyer. The consequences of the Maria Colwell case surely points to the need to listen to the child. Indeed, the subsequent enquiry into this case stressed the importance of communicating with children. Given this degree of recognition and the recent progress in providing representation for children, professional (including legal) opinion should not adopt the repressive step of silencing and overriding children's views. On the evidence it seems that Maria Colwell was right and the professionals were wrong.

8
Legal Rights and Treatment Bureaucracy

The concept of 'childhood' has fascinated a wide range of professional groups, many with conflicting views and aims but all struggling to influence the child's development. Victor Hugo's remark 'I have discovered the child' could well epitomise our generation. According to David Owen, Minister of State in the Department of Health and Social Security, there was no shortage of advice to the Government in the preparation of the Children Bill in 1975, and during 1979 some 500 children's organisations became affiliated to the British International Year of the Child Association. This multiplicity of organisations epitomises the concern for children which has developed over the past 100 years. Along with this increased awareness of the importance of childhood, there has been increased emphasis on children's rights. But 'children's rights' are an emotive and equivocal issue. Debate often no more than conceals society's intervention with the lives of children in accordance with its *own* terms.

In this chapter we examine some non-judicial decisions made in relation to children and highlight those areas in which justice appears to have been side-stepped in the so-called 'best interests' or 'welfare' of the child. Many of these decisions are socially and politically sensitive, and are personally and emotionally important for the well-being of the child. Yet the administrative procedures which deal with the future of children have evolved in a somewhat casual and fragmentary way.

What is in a child's 'best interests' frequently conforms with social and political expediency. Public conscience has been constantly appeased through committees of inquiry and legislation (of which the Ingleby Committee and the 1975 Children Act are recent examples) which have, in fact, changed little. The 1975 Children Act was the result of pressure from competing interest groups which focused *around* the child rather than legislated *for* the child.

The reorganisation of the social services following the Seebohm Committee report facilitated the creation of a bureaucracy within which professional opinion flourishes. What is in the 'best interests' of a child may differ in each case, and is incapable of precise formulation; usually it is determined by professional opinion. But professional discretion and decision-making are not infallible or immune from misuse. This means that decisions made by professionals about children in their 'best interests' should be more open to public accountability and scrutiny; decision-making is often hidden behind a smoke-screen of professional omnipotence and bureaucratic procedure. When a case finally comes to court, decisions which determine the outcome may already have been taken. Wardship proceedings, for example, can take so long that a child can remain with foster parents for a considerable length of time before the case is fully heard in the High Court. Even though it might be discovered from the evidence that the child was wrongly removed from his natural parents, the Judge might decide that the child is so settled with the foster parents that, in the 'best interests' of the child, he should remain with them. The 'best interests' cliché permeates the child care profession – in child abuse registers, juvenile court procedures, decisions to place a child in the care of the local authority and so on. In this chapter we examine a few issues which highlight areas in which arbitrary and unjust decisions can occur – proceedings under the 1948 Children Act, abuse registers and case conferences, and the lack of rights among children in care.

From voluntary to involuntary care

In 1977 there were 36,800 admissions of children to care under section 1 of the 1948 Act. The spirit of the Act is reflected in a Home Office circular dated 8 July 1948. It stated:

> While the provisions of this Act relate only to children who have had the misfortune to be deprived of a normal home life, the importance must also be kept in mind of doing all that is possible to save children suffering this misfortune . . . To keep the family together must be the first aim. The separation of the child from his

parents can only be justified when there is no possibility of securing adequate care for a child in his own home (Home Office Circular No. 160/1948, 8 July 1948).

It was clear from subsequent practice that children were not always being received into care as a last resort. Indeed, the fact that children were being received into care because of parental homelessness or financial and material hardship led a Government committee to recommend in 1960 that local authorities should have a general duty to prevent or forestall the suffering of children through neglect in their own homes and to provide material resources for these families. This recommendation was enacted in the Children and Young Persons Act 1963.

But this did not prevent a substantial number of children coming into voluntary care. Poverty, marital separation and homelessness continue to be contributory factors to these admissions. According to the National Council for One Parent Families, over half of the children currently in care come from one-parent families. The decision whether or not to offer financial or material assistance as an alternative to receiving a child into care lies within the discretion of local-authority social service departments, and this may depend on the individual social worker's view of the parents and their ability to cope with the child. In one case we know of a social worker refused a single-parent father's request for a child-minder for his young baby and instigated care proceedings instead.

Although section 1 does not grant a local authority the right to retain a child, parents seeking the return of their child may not find it easy. Research shows that parents are not regularly seen by social workers. Thorpe, for example, found that 45 per cent of her couples had not been seen by a social worker for a least 2 years and Holman's research showed that neither mother nor father had been visited by a social worker for at least a year in 54 per cent of his sample of local authority cases. In Thorpe's sample 62 per cent of the parents did not know where their children had been placed, and 72 per cent of the children had had no contact with their parents. Return to the family was being actively considered in only 5 per cent of the cases. Thorpe also found that 70 per cent of the parents were coping well with the other children in their family. This means that parents can lose their children through default of the social worker rather than their own fault.

The language of the 1948 Act is in some aspects confusing. For example, the provision which requires that the return of the child to his family should be consistent with his welfare seems at odds with the local authority's otherwise mandatory duty to return the child on the request of the parents. Until recently judicial authority on this point was unclear; different cases resulted in inconsistent decisions, with no clear guiding principles for local authorities and the courts. While some local authorities felt that they had a residual discretion to retain care of the child, others returned the child on request.

In one case Lord Goddard said that 'the local authority *must* hand the child to a parent'. In a later case, however, a father who demanded the return of his 17-year-old daughter was unsuccessful. The girl was with foster parents with whom she wished to stay. The Court of Appeal realised the impracticality of making the girl move against her will and held that the local authority had, in fact, no mandatory duty to return the girl to her father. In another case a mother who wished to regain care of her child was also unsuccessful. Lord Widgery decided that only a *fit* parent could demand the return of his child, but this reasoning is muddled, and both the Court of Appeal and House of Lords have held it to be incorrect. The test of parental fitness refers only to circumstances which justify a local authority assuming full parental rights; parental unfitness does not disqualify a parent from removing the child from voluntary care.

The Children Act 1975, which could have clarified these inconsistencies, instead increased the confusion. Parents now have to give 28 days' notice if they wish to remove their child from the care of the local authority where the child has been in care for more than 6 months. This was designed to prevent abrupt removal of the child from care and to give the local authority breathing space so that it could make a planned return home or take legal action (such as the assumption of parental rights) in instances in which it thought that the child should not return to the parents. The 6-month limit was reached by a combination of pressure group action and parliamentary compromise; 28 days is also an arbitrary period and it has caused difficulties. On the one hand, many social workers view it as too short to re-establish children with their families in a planned way; on the other hand, some local authorities who are unsure about the desirability of returning a child quickly to his parents have sought parental rights over a child in order to avoid this.

A recent case highlights these difficulties. A baby girl was received into voluntary care and placed in foster care. The mother later telephoned the local-authority social services department requesting her return, but 5 weeks later the local authority passed a section 2 resolution. When the mother objected, the case was referred to the juvenile court for confirmation of the resolution. The court refused to accept jurisdiction on the grounds that the mother's phone call had terminated 'voluntary care' and that the child was no longer legally in voluntary care. This point was, however, subsequently successfully appealed to the House of Lords in another case. Local authorities can now pass section 2 resolutions during the 28-day breathing space even when parents have notified them that they wish the child to be returned to them. But the House of Lords decision is unclear in respect of the child who has been in care less than 6 months. It seems that the local authority must either hand the child back or instigate wardship proceedings, since there is no right to retain the child indefinitely after a request for his return has been made.

It may seem reasonable for local authorities to have the power to extend the use of section 2 resolutions to the period after which parents have requested the return of their child from voluntary care, but these resolutions were not meant to be used in this way. In fact such use defeats its purpose, which is to provide the child with a substitute parent only after *careful assessment and consideration* has assured that further care is in the child's best interest. The passing of section 2 resolutions in order to prolong the 28-day breathing space indefinitely is highly suspect. Where parents do object and go on to win the case in the juvenile court, it may be many months before the child is returned to them. In certain parts of the country it takes up to 3 months to obtain a date for a full hearing in the juvenile court, and during this period the local authority retains the care and control of the child.

On 31 March 1977 16,300 children were the subjects of section 2 resolutions, with the parental rights and duties vested in the local authority. The major proportion of these were the result of informal and administrative rather than formal and judicial decisions. Only about 10 per cent of these resolutions are objected to and are adjudicated in the juvenile court. Failure to object is not necessarily clear evidence that the parents accept the grounds or that the criteria for passing a resolution are met. This lack of judicial scrutiny means that there is, at least, the possibility of error and abuse in these decisions.

First, parents have no right to be forewarned of the local authority's intention to assume parental rights: the decision is made behind the closed doors of the social services department and council chamber upon information supplied by the social services department. The letter of notification is formal and might well be received by parents at a time of stress and difficulty. Since there is no obligation on the local authority to ensure that a personal visit is made by a social worker to the parents in order to explain the letter of notification, the possibility remains that the contents of the letter and the consequences flowing from it may not be fully appreciated. Some parents may not be able to read, let alone comprehend the contents of the letter. Parents who do not appreciate the consequences of the letter may fail to object to the passing of the resolution. Secondly, the onus of notifying the parents lies with the local authority, but only if the whereabouts of the parents are known. Parents place children into voluntary care for a number of reasons and not all appreciate the need to keep the local authority constantly notified of any change of address. The local authority, on the other hand, may not make sufficient efforts to trace parents. The following case history serves as an example of this.

Joan W., after increasingly violent attacks by her husband, decided to leave him, and so placed her four children in the care of a London borough while she tried to obtain another home. Eventually she was given a one-bedroomed flat by the housing department. When she applied for a larger house, she was told that it was not necessary as her children were in care. After a week-end visit from one son, Joan decided to keep him with her. When Joan's husband moved out of their old flat, she moved in and then applied to the social services department for the return of her other three children. Joan was told that the children had been made subjects of a section 2 resolution and that she could not have them back. The social worker had not notified Joan of this at the time, and claimed that she had not been able to trace Joan W. This claim does not stand up to examination, as Joan had kept constantly in touch with her children while they were in care.

Lack of contact by a parent, for whatever reason, for whatever length of time, enables the local authority to pass a section 2 resolution without the parent receiving the required notification. This can cause difficulties. Many children, for example, come into voluntary care because a parent is admitted to a psychiatric hospital. It may take considerable time for a full recovery to be made, yet resolutions can be passed while a parent is in hospital and is unable to object. On recovery, a parent may find it difficult to obtain discharge of the care order. Even where parents do object to the resolution, they are at a considerable disadvantage in obtaining information about the reasons relied on by the local authority in passing the resolution. A recent case (The Times Law Report, 10 May 1977) highlights this.

A mother applied to the juvenile court for discharge of a section 2 resolution over her children. The issue was whether or not the resolution was in the children's interests, and the mother's lawyers sought and obtained from the juvenile court a summons to force the Director of Social Services to appear at the hearing with all the case records. The mother's lawyer intended to extract from the records any information supportive of the mother's case and to discover why the local authority was objecting to the mother's application.

The local authority appealed against the juvenile court's decision that the documents were not privileged. The Divisional Court quashed the decision, but not on the ground that the documents were privileged. It held rather that there was simply no procedure for the discovery of such documents in the magistrates' courts. However, Lord Widgery, the Lord Chief Justice, felt that such documents *ought* to have been open to review and challenge. He said: 'It revolted the sense of justice that local authorities should hold all the documents while the parents had access to none.' Currently parents do not have the right to know the nature of the objections they have to meet.

None of us can be sure that at all times we act with complete integrity and infallibility. For this reason, safeguards are necessary. But the actual mechanism by which a section 2 resolution is obtained is very simple and depends very much on the quality of the individual social worker and local-authority social services department. The criteria for obtaining a section 2 resolution are often subjective; they depend on the social worker's perception of the family. This is shaped by a number of factors: the social worker's personality and training, the structure and morale of the social services department, and the social worker's relationship with the parent and child. There is no objective standard by which parents can be assessed as 'bad parents'. Such an assessment can be as much a product of a clash of personalities as of the parents' behaviour. Social enquiry reports are often scattered with such inexact terms as 'manipulative', 'aggressive', 'inadequate', 'schizoid', and 'infantile'. Even in trained hands psychological concepts can be misused, and there is an even greater risk that this might happen when young and untrained social workers prepare reports.

The reports prepared to support a section 2 resolution are often short, not more than a few hundred words, and they are referred to the social services committee of the local authority council, which usually rubber stamps them (unless there is some policy decision not to pass resolutions on certain grounds). It is rare for such resolutions to be rejected. Of course, it is difficult for a committee, consisting mainly of councillors with little or no social work background, to look critically at such reports, especially when there is no contradictory report from the parents or their representatives. The following case history is an example of the dependence of the social services committee on the information provided by the social worker.

An illegitimate boy was abandoned by his mother within his first year and was subsequently brought up by his putative father. When the boy was 8 years old, his father committed suicide and the boy was received into care under section 1 of the Children Act 1948. At this time the sister of the child's father and her husband made it clear to the social services department that they wished to have care of the child, so that he could be brought up with their four children. The local authority refused this request and fostered the child with the fiancée of the child's father, who had been living with him for only a short time before his death. She was a single woman and had no children of her own. A section 2 resolution was passed on the child on the grounds that his mother had abandoned him. The uncle and aunt then began wardship proceedings. The Official Solicitor was appointed to act for the child and the local authority made no objection to this or to his subsequent investigations. The Official Solicitor's recommendations supported the application of the aunt and uncle. When the case was heard, the local authority argued that this was a matter for its discretion, which was clearly vested in it by statute, and not one in which the High Court could exercise its jurisdiction through wardship proceedings. The High Court Judge decided that, although *prima facie* local authorities' decisions about a child in care were a matter for individual local authorities, he would hear the merits of the case for two reasons: first, the Official Solicitor's view was diametrically opposed to that of the local authority and, secondly, the social services committee of the council which passed the resolution had insufficient information in the social work report to enable it to exercise its statutory discretion properly. The social work report had failed to make any mention of the existence of the paternal relatives and of their wish to care for the child. The Judge felt that the social services committee should have gone beyond deciding whether or not grounds existed (that the mother had abandoned the child), and that it should have considered the practical consequences of assuming parental rights and powers and the alternatives to it. The Judge decided that, in this case, the local authority had not exercised its discretion properly.

The High Court, however, rarely interferes with such areas of discretion. In general there is little judicial scrutiny. This, and the lack of social work accountability, makes certain children and families vulnerable to state intervention.

Child abused: the collection of information

The death of Maria Colwell, aged 7, at the hands of her stepfather in 1973 caused considerable public reaction. The resulting inquiry created the impression that the helping agencies, especially social services, had failed in their task to protect Maria Colwell from becoming a battered child. Her death provoked a massive response from the DHSS, social services departments and medical authorities. Child abuse became a central, some would say a dominating, concern in the fieldwork social services as further deaths of children at the hands of their parents received widespread press publicity. Battered children were good copy, and social workers bore the consequences.

The Report of the Committee of Inquiry into the 'Care and Supervision Provided in Relation to Maria Colwell' stated in its conclusions that the major failing of the agencies dealing with Maria and her family was the lack of communication and liaison. Social services, the NSPCC, the school, the housing department and the police were all at some time or other concerned with the case, and yet there was no attempt to co-ordinate their activities. In consequence vital information about Maria's physical and emotional state failed to be passed on. There was also confusion as to which of the agencies had primary responsibility for the family. This failure of communication was central to other well publicised cases of child abuse, such as that of Lisa Godfrey, who was killed by her mother in October 1973. The Report of that Committee of Inquiry stated:

> Whether the life of Lisa Godfrey could have been safeguarded without her removal from her home had there been better co-ordination between the Social, the Probation, the Medical and Health Services can only be a matter of opinion. There can be no doubt, however, that, if co-ordination and communication between these services had been effective then on the information and evidence available to one or more of the services, the degree of risk of repeated serious non-accidental injury to Lisa should have been clearly recognised and acted upon (Lambeth, Southwark and Lewisham Area Health Authority, etc., 1975, p. 3).

By 1973 there was widespread recognition of the 'battered child syndrome'. Henry Kempe, a paediatrician at the University of Colorado School of Medicine, had in the early sixties coined this phrase to define the child who was physically abused by his parents. There was a great rush of research on both sides of the Atlantic to assess whether or not there were predictive signs in the family which could help professional workers in identifying the child who was abused or was 'at risk' of abuse. Many researchers felt there were such predictive signs and that, therefore, a central register with the names of those children 'at risk' should be created. Professional workers could then be called on to investigate a family because of a neighbour's complaint that the parents were physically ill-treating their child, and could check whether or not there was any evidence of the child having been abused on an earlier occasion. Such registers were set up in all states in the U.S.A. by the late sixties.

After the deaths in Britain the DHSS issued a memorandum on 'non-accidental injury to children' in April 1974, which was sent to all Area Health Authorities and Directors of Social Services. It set out guidelines to be followed in dealing with cases of non-accidental injury, and it was no surprise that this included instructions on the setting up of local procedures aimed at improving communication and aiding liaison between the different agencies. The use of case conferences and the initiation of registers in each Area Health Authority were central to the operation of the new procedures.

The guidelines suggested how the procedures would operate at the local level. A case conference was to be called as soon as the local authority was notified that a child had suffered or was thought to have suffered a non-accidental injury. The case conference was to consist of representatives from a variety of agencies, including social services, health services, the educational department if the child was of school age, and any other professional and voluntary agencies which were involved with the child and/or family. (Initially the police were invited only at the discretion of the convenor of the case conference, but this practice has now changed and police are usually present.) The guidelines suggested that the case conference should decide whether or not further action should be taken, and, if so, who should be appointed as key worker with the family and child and to liaise with the other agencies. It has become standard practice for the first case conference to decide whether or not the child's name should be placed on the abuse register.

Initially the guidelines seemed reasonable and gave hope that further tragedies could be avoided or the number greatly reduced. On a number of counts, however, the guidelines and the way in which they have been implemented have had serious and disturbing side-effects, especially in the field of civil liberties.

There is wide variation in the criteria used by Area Review Committees for placing children on the register. Some authorities only place children on the register if the injury is proved to have been non-accidentally inflicted. Though it is not always possible for doctors to differentiate between non-accidental and accidental injury, at least medical criteria are likely to be objectively based. This contrasts with the criteria for determining whether or not a child is 'at risk'. Because 'at risk' is such a nebulous concept (often taking in the whole gamut of social, economic, and psychological factors), the subjective impressions of the case-conference participants of the child and his family may well decide whether or not the child is placed on the register. As professional anxiety tends to be high in the area of child abuse, the child is usually placed on the register once a conference is called. Until he is taken off the register, there will be regular conferences to discuss the family and child, often without their knowledge.

As the British Association of Social Workers points out in its publication *The Central Child Abuse Register*, these registers could easily drift 'into an overburdened and increasingly irrelevant list of children about whom professionals are concerned'. According to Martin and Schneider's research, around 25 per cent of all parents provide parenting which could be criticised from some professional viewpoint or other, often as the result of a mixture of environmental and social pressures and personality characteristics. A large number of children and parents may, therefore, end up on the register simply because of some contact with social services or other agencies. A mother, for example, may have gone to the social services for material help, and the social worker may, on meeting the mother and visiting the home, feel that the children are 'at risk'. A case conference may then be called and the children placed on the register. Neither the parent nor the child have any right of appeal against the latter's name being placed on the register. They may not even know.

One injustice is often compounded by another. There is no statutory obligation placed on social services departments to inform the parents either that a case conference is to be called or of the placement of their child on the register. Both the British Association of Social Workers and the National Council of Civil Liberties find this a disturbing aspect of the present procedures, and stressed, in their evidence to the Select Committee on Violence in the Family, that on both professional and civil-liberty grounds parents should be informed that their child has been placed on the register. In its report the Select Committee recommended that parents should normally be informed when this happens, but this recommendation has largely been ignored. Parents in most areas are not told of their child's placement on the register. It is estimated that up to 90 per cent of parents with children on the register have no knowledge that this has occurred.

Even where parents have been informed that there is to be a case conference, they have no right of representation at it. The case conference is not a court of law, although allegations are made against parents and 'judgements' are passed. In our experience false allegations are made about parents' behaviour and then circulated to all the agencies present at the case conference in the case-conference minutes. Miss M, for example, was said by the health visitor to be a prostitute. She based her allegations on the fact that Miss M had children by four different fathers and that the house was too well furnished for Miss M to be simply living on Social Security payments. No one present was able to refute this allegation, and so it was recorded in the case-conference minutes. Later the social worker in the case was able to show that the allegation was false, but by then this allegation against Miss M's character had already affected people's judgement of her ability to care for her children and had led to speculation on the damage that this was causing the children. The information had also been widely circulated to a number of agencies and institutions, including the children's schools.

Such allegations and opinions can remain in the files of schools, social services departments, health authorities, police and other agencies for many years, and can affect the perception of the agencies and personnel who are working with the child and family. Once a family is labelled in a particular way, subsequent actions are often interpreted to fit those labels. Hence a minor injury to the child can result in care proceedings where the family has already been labelled as 'at risk' even though no previous injuries have occurred. This, in fact, happened to Miss M. Though there had never been any evidence of the children having been abused, they were placed on the register, as the family was considered to be 'at risk'. Sometime later Miss M admitted to the social worker that she had hit her youngest child on the leg. It was a very minor injury. The skin of the boy's leg had not been broken though there was superficial bruising. The child was made the subject of a place of safety order and later a full care order was made under the 1969 Children and Young Persons Act. This would probably not have happened if the children had not already been on the abuse register.

If the case conference makes the decision to apply for a care order, this can put the parents and child at a considerable disadvantage when the case comes to court, because many of the professionals in court to give evidence will have been present at the case conference at which much of the evidence to be presented has already been discussed. In addition, the professional's opinion, often enshrined in reports for the court, is more likely to reflect the case-conference decision rather than be an independent assessment of the child and family.

Considerable controversy has arisen over the position of the police in cases of non-accidental injury. In 1976 a joint DHSS/Home Office circular pressed for closer co-operation between the police and other agencies. Indeed, there have recently been further suggestions that the police should attend a broader range of case conferences concerning children 'at risk' than at present. But this trend infringes basic civil liberties.

First, the police are under an obligation to investigate any alleged offence coming to their notice and, therefore, cannot undertake not to prosecute in individual cases. This means that the police could take action independently of the case conference they have attended: for example, initiate legal proceedings, civil or criminal. This may be at odds with the views of the case conference. According to Peter Morris, it is not unusual for evidence of criminality to arise at case conferences. A social worker may know, for example, that an unmarried mother supplements her income from social security by casual prostitution. Such a statement may place his client at risk of prosecution if police officers are present at the case conference.

Secondly, the police have one of the most sophisticated information computer systems in this country. Families who are discussed at non-accidental injury case conferences at which the police are present may have the details of their circumstances recorded by the police and possibly held on the central Scotland Yard index. Joanna Buckle writes:

> Given the reality that, in the majority of cases where a child is presenting with injuries the cause of which are never fully ascertained, and indeed in some cases which may be genuinely accidental or the result of some organic deficiency (brittle bones), police recording of such matters would appear a gross infringement of civil liberties (Buckle, p. 25).

With all this information collected and recorded on children and families, it is not surprising that the confidentiality of such information has become a burning issue for policy-makers, those operating the system, and the many pressure groups in this area. It is extraordinary that children and parents have no right to know what information has been recorded about them in numerous filing systems and that professional groups have easy access to this information. The British Association of Social Workers (in its publication *The Central Child Abuse Register*) points out that in the vast majority of areas not only social workers have easy access to the register but also such groups as doctors, police and teachers. Mr. Jones, (a member of the British Association of Social Workers' group giving evidence to the Select Committee on Violence in the Family) claimed that in some areas information could be obtained by people who simply rang up and claimed to be social workers.

As yet there is no uniform method for removing a child's name from the 'abuse' register, though the DHSS has suggested a new procedure. But whatever bureaucratic method is implemented, it is likely that most local authorities will keep a second register of 'inactive cases' – those cases on which it is no longer felt necessary to hold case conferences.

In addition to central 'abuse' registers, there are often registers in each local authority as well as in hospitals and police stations. Some local authorities further increase the confusion by dividing the register into categories of high, medium and low risk. Yet placing a child's name on the register is not based on scientific or administratively clear criteria, but on the subjective opinion of the case conference.

The original purpose of these registers was to improve communication between different agencies and to provide information at some central point in order to prevent such tragedies as the death of Maria Colwell. But the plethora of registers, and the inability to be clear on the criteria upon which children should be placed on them, have created a large and expensive bureaucratic structure which seriously threatens the civil liberties of parents and children. According to the DHSS, the average cost of a case conference is £180. It is difficult to calculate how many children are on the abuse registers nationally but it is likely to be at least 50,000 children. The DHSS specified in its latest circular that children on the abuse register should be reviewed every 4 months, which means that the cost of keeping such registers is about £27 million a year. This cost in time and money is disturbing, because it inevitably decreases the amount of time and money available for preventive work with children and their families. Furthermore, it is not clear that the registers do prevent children being beaten or abused. So far as it is possible to ascertain, there is no appreciable decline in the number of children being abused (and, of course, the number of cases not known to the various concerned agencies is likely to be very high).

This has not led to local authorities and the DHSS reassessing the use of abuse registers. In fact it is now suggested that children thought to be in danger of suffering physical, mental or emotional abuse of a degree which *could* lead to their being placed on the 'abuse register' *should* be placed on it. This is nirvana for those who believe that human behaviour can be predicted successfully. But, as Jan Didrichsen writes:

> At the moment there is no behavioural science which can predict human behaviour with certainty . . . We simply do not know, nor are we ever likely to know, enough about human affairs to make such a prediction (Didrichsen, 1979, p. 14).

The creation of child-abuse registers and procedures assumes otherwise. It is increasingly likely that more and more children and parents will be labelled, written and talked about, and filed for posterity with no right of appeal or, necessarily, the knowledge that it is happening.

Who cares?

In March 1977 there were 101,250 children in care in England and Wales. Of these, 34,000 were in foster care, 18,000 were in the charge of a parent, guardian, relative or friend and 33,700 were in community homes; 42,000 children had spent more than 3 years in care and a further 33,400 children had spent between 1 and 3 years in care. These children are potentially the most vulnerable in our society.

Once parental powers have been vested in the local authority, there is no external accountability for the authority's decisions or actions except in the rare occasions on which the local Ombudsman is called in to investigate maladministration. An individual child's future in care largely rests with his social worker, residential staff and/or his foster parents. In the words of Fitzherbert, 'A child can escape from negligent parents by being taken into care, but there is no escape from a negligent social worker' (Fitzherbert, 1976, p. 36).

There is general agreement that once a child is taken into care, he should not be moved. Yet national figures suggest that frequent changes in placement are normal for most children. Yule and Raynes found in their sample that 11 per cent of the children had had one placement and that 85 per cent had had between two and five placements. (A further 4 per cent had had between six and ten placements.)

Some local authorities exacerbate the movement problem through their rigid system of receiving children into care. For example, a child is usually first placed with short-term foster parents or in a residential institution. Next he is placed in the local observation and assessment centre, for a period that can vary from a few months to more than a year. 'Experts' then decide what is the most suitable placement for the child, but this decision often depends on what is available rather than what is 'ideal'. These so-called 'planned' placements often break down, especially placements in foster care. One child described how his foster placement began: 'When I was fostered, I hadn't even met the foster parents. I wasn't even told I was going there until they said, 'Put your coat on. We're going . . . ' (*Who Cares?*, p. 46). Of all foster placements of children aged 5 or more, 78 per cent fail. The National Child Development Study (Pringle, 1975) has also shown that by the age of seven 60 per cent of all children in care have already experienced foster care. Of these, 53 per cent had been in two foster homes and 8 per cent in three or more. Such changes of placement are common experiences for children in care. As one boy said: 'I'm terrified to see my social worker. Every time I do I change children's home' (Foster, 1977, p. 3).

The protection of children's rights once in care goes far deeper than the question of placement. It is widely accepted that residential care is rarely a satisfactory environment for children to grow up in. The quality of residential staff and the duration of their stay in children's homes are crucial factors in creating a stable and caring environment. Newman, however, found in a survey of 65 children's homes that half were understaffed. The national turnover rate of residential staff in 1971 was between 30 and 40 per cent, and it is unlikely that this has improved substantially since then. The majority of residential staff have also received little training. A MIND survey, published in 1975, found that only 13 per cent of residential staff were trained.

Children in care also have numerous changes in their field social worker. In the words of one boy:

> My brother and I have had more social workers than I can remember. They'd see us once and then disappear for six months, then we'd have a new one. And it's been going on all the time I've been in the home. They've been leaving or they've been ill. And if that's happening all the time, I don't see how they can help you (*Who Cares?*, p. 29).

Various Acts relating to children in care have made it clear that local authorities have a statutory duty to hold 6-monthly reviews of the child's need to be in care. A review should be the forum at which people concerned with the child discuss his progress and plans for the future. As far as possible the child's wishes should be ascertained and made clear at the review meeting. A growing number of groups, including the 'Voice of the Child in Care' and 'Who Cares?' have been critical of the review procedure. They state that decisions about a child are frequently taken without consulting him, and that it is rare for children to be invited to participate in their review even when they are over the age of 11.

The unsatisfactory nature of reviews was highlighted by a report prepared by Nottinghamshire Social Services Department in 1975, which, in a survey of 550 children in residential care, found that 36 per cent were inappropriately placed, 26 per cent could have returned home or have been fostered, and that the reviews had not prepared long-term plans. The report concluded that although some reviews had been thorough, others had been 'superficial and cursory'.

Decisions supposedly made to promote the 'best interests' of the child can become immune from change. The bureaucratic procedure by which placement and review decisions are taken do not provide a critical appraisal of all the issues in the case. The privileged legal status of local-authority social services departments provides them with wide powers (through indeterminate care orders) and discretion. Those in care have little voice.

9
New Directions: a Family Court

The juvenile court is an inadequate forum for adjudicating complex civil matters concerning children and their families; the welfare ethos of the court has placed a low priority on the legal rights of those affected by its jurisdiction. There is also considerable uncertainty about the notion of 'welfare'. Child-care literature shows that there are no agreed values on the socialisation of children. A review of existing studies on techniques for predicting long-term harm to children on the basis of parental behaviour led Harvard psychologist Sheldon White to conclude:

> Neither theory nor research has specified the exact mechanisms by which a child's development and his family functioning are linked. While speculation abounds, there is little agreement about how these family functions produce variations in measures of health, learning and affect. Nor do we know the relative importance of internal (individual and family) versus external (social and economic) factors (White, 1973, p. 240).

Nevertheless the existing powers and wide discretion of juvenile courts and social services departments are based on the assumption that these agencies do have sufficient 'knowledge' to make such decisions as whether or not a child should be removed from home. Except in the case of immediate serious injury or danger, removal of the child from home may be more harmful than beneficial: to be separated from a familiar environment can be psychologically traumatic and damaging to a child; but the present child-care system cannot guarantee a stable and secure upbringing to a child removed from his home. Yet contemporary British society makes it as difficult as possible for parents to keep their child when they run into difficulties. To remedy this, we suggest a new direction for intervention in the lives of children and their families.

Towards a family court

Intervention by the state into parental rights and responsibilities, like the reallocation of rights within the family, properly belongs to family law and should come within the aegis of a court which has comprehensive jurisdiction over family matters. The juvenile court is primarily concerned with the position of children, and yet its procedures have placed a low priority on their rights and those of their family. Improvement of these procedures would not enable the juvenile court to assume the features of a family court, since, apart from adoption and care proceedings, the juvenile court has little experience of adjudicating other aspects of family crisis. Matters affecting families are currently scattered across the magistrates' courts, the County Courts and the High Court; the choice of jurisdiction is determined by procedural rules and, in some circumstances, by the applicant in the proceedings. Issues relating to children can be heard in all three of these courts, each of which, arguably, could assume the civil care jurisdiction of the juvenile courts. We recommend the creation of a family court with comprehensive powers over *all* aspects of family crisis (other than criminal matters).

The report of the Finer Committee provides a useful discussion of the type of forum we envisage. It recommended the creation of a judicial institution 'which in dealing with family matters does justice according to the law'. Its fundamental assumption was that 'the object of achieving welfare must not be permitted to weaken or short-cut the normal safeguards of the judicial process'. Because notions of 'welfare' conflict with notions of justice and expressions of 'welfare' can carry risks as well as benefits, the Committee recommended that there should be a clear distinction between the court's welfare and adjudicatory process. Accordingly, it suggested that the court should be governed by procedures which promote an orderly and fair hearing, with examination of evidence properly adduced and the availability of representation to all parties concerned in the case. This new court would not see the parties who come before it as 'clients' or as 'patients' for whom the court process is one form of, or preliminary to, treatment. In the words of the Committee, the aim of the family court must be to ensure that the individual remains '*the subject of rights* not *the object of assistance*'.

In considering the structure of the court, the report recommended that there should be two tiers. The first was to be local and presided over by a County Court Judge; the second was to be the present Family Division of the High Court presided over by a High Court Judge. The Family Division would provide the link to the Court of Appeal and the House of Lords. All cases would start at the local level, with difficult matters and appeals on points of law being referred to the High Court tier. An intermediate tier was also proposed for dealing with appeals on fact from the local tier. We agree with this structure. The essential feature of an easily accessible local court is that it would provide speedy and cheap determination of cases.

Judges in the family court should possess a broad knowledge of the various welfare services available to families in stress. The local tier Judge would be drawn from current County Court Judges and from lawyers currently specialising in the various branches of family law. The Finer Committee recommended that he should be assisted by two members of the lay magistracy drawn from a panel with special interest or expertise in family matters. We agree with this, as such a tribunal would combine legal skills with sensitivity to the effects of family breakdown.

Our proposals for intervention are based on criteria which have no recourse to the 'best interests' test currently prevalent in the hearing of cases which affect children. This is an unsatisfactory principle, which relies on subjective interpretation. We propose instead principles which, we believe, will greatly reduce the numbers of cases requiring to be formally dealt with in the family courts and will, therefore, provide a higher quality of care and protection to those children brought before the court. The principles are interrelated and, as such, must be read together.

The principle of respect for family autonomy

Commentary

Parental autonomy in child-rearing must be respected. Diversity of views and life-styles means that families raise children in a wide variety of living situations (for example, communes and extended, nuclear or single-parent families). Child-rearing practices also vary over time and in different classes, races and religious groups. This may be the product of conscious choice (for example, the child-rearing practices of Jehovah's Witnesses or orthodox Jews). Here intervention carries a substantial risk of 'saving' children from families who merely have different life-styles from dominant conceptions of appropriate child-rearing. But there is no 'proper' way to raise children. Designations such as 'good' or 'poor' homes are subjective notions. Indeed Cicourel has suggested that judgements by social workers and courts on families are biased against lower-class families; middle-class families provide the model for what a 'good' home should be. Certainly research has shown that the children of one-parent families are more frequently removed from them than from two-parent families. According to the National Council of One Parent Families, over half of the children in care in 1978 were from one-parent families. Holman has argued that while the poor are handicapped by their circumstances and inadequate resources from meeting their children's needs, society expects from them the same practices of family life and child care as more privileged groups. Similarly Titmuss, writing some years ago, stressed that 'in the pursuit of what is called "higher standards of child care," there is the danger of assuming that the norms of one social class are relevant to the needs of another'. But, as Wilson and Herbert's research found: 'Material shortages in the home and poor environmental conditions severely affect child-rearing methods. Life in the slum forces parents to adopt methods of child-rearing they do not approve of.' Intervention in these cases penalises those who are already disadvantaged. A Bengali boy who had ricketts, for example, was removed from his family on the grounds of abuse and neglect. It was only on appeal that a second medical opinion that ricketts was a common disease among Asians and reflected the family's social circumstances rather than deliberate abuse or neglect was accepted.

The promotion by local-authority social services departments of particular child-care practices and their monitoring of a child's development should take place only on a voluntary basis. Intervention by the state should only occur when a child is suffering from specifically defined harm.

Practice

Every child must have the basic right of remaining in his own family unless there are compelling reasons which justify his removal. This presumption in favour of parental autonomy should only be rebutted on proof of some *specific* harm to the child or of the disruption or absence of parental ties. Even where this is proved, however, there should be a presumption against removal of the child from his home; such intervention should be a last resort. Removal should require a thorough survey of alternative ways of dealing with the situation (for example, by voluntary services and support) and evidence that such measures are inadequate. State services should aim at encouraging and strengthening the resources of families. When intervention is authorised, every attempt should be made to rectify the particular situation which has resulted in harm to the child, so that, wherever possible, the child can be rehabilitated into the family.

The principle of voluntary services

Commentary

Insufficient emphasis is currently placed on keeping children in their families. Holman, for example, has shown that the financial provision made available by the 1963 Children and Young Persons Act in order to prevent children being received into care is under-used. There must be a wide range of social work and other services which seek to support families: nurseries, day-care centres, play centres and so on. The largest category of children received into voluntary care in 1977 was the result of the short-term illness of a parent (11,500), and there is some indication that poverty and environmental influences still account for many receptions into care: in 1977 5,800 children came into care because of unsatisfactory home conditions, 1,300 children because of homelessness and some 6,000 were the children of single parents who were unable to cope alone. While some parents will always be unable to cope, many others could manage if some support service (for example, day-time care) was available to them. Yet the number of places in day nurseries decreased from 65,000 just after the Second World War to 25,000 in 1975.

There will continue to be circumstances in which parents will require to place their children in voluntary care. Currently these procedures are informal, but can result in local authorities retaining children in care contrary to the parents' wishes. Such decisions require judicial scrutiny.

Practice

Before a child is taken into voluntary care, every effort should be made to explore alternative courses of action, including the provision of material assistance. If voluntary reception into care is the *only available* option, the parties should enter into a formal agreement whereby the rights and obligations of each member are set out. This should include a statement that the parents agree to the reception into care and that all realistic alternatives have been explored, and should specify the parents' rights of access to the child and their right to have the child returned to them within 48 hours of notifying the social services department. Where a child has remained in voluntary care for 6 months, the situation must be reviewed by the court in order to assess the continued case for the child remaining in care and to examine alternatives. If, after 18 months, the child is still in care and the parents have severed all contact with him, the court may, at its discretion, vest parental rights and powers with the local authority. This would be precluded, however, unless the local authority presents to the court plans (acceptable to the court and to a specially appointed 'guardian *ad litem*') for the long-term non-institutional placement of the child.

The principle of limited intervention in the lives of children and families

Commentary

Currently the juvenile court has wide jurisdiction over children who have not committed offences. In 1977 1,100 children were taken into care because they were 'truants', 200 as in 'moral danger' and 500 as 'beyond parental control'. We recommend that this jurisdiction be abolished; courts are inadequate agencies for dealing with such matters.

Truancy has primarily been viewed as a personal failing on the part of the juvenile or, on occasions, as a symptom of pathological disorder in the family. Schools have rarely, either in theory or practice, looked for explanations of truancy in terms of their own deficiencies. Yet Michael Rutter's recent study shows clearly that certain schools with a similar intake had much higher truancy rates than other schools. Rutter goes on to show that the reasons for this lie within the individual schools rather than with the pupils. The relevance of the present educational system is rarely questioned; similarly the content of formal education often does not, in any real way, relate to the life experiences of many schoolchildren. This results in less academic pupils becoming bored or frustrated. Because reform of the education system (making it of interest and relevance to everyone) takes money, time and thought and could disrupt present institutions, it is more convenient to deal with truancy in individual terms and avoid the many political issues which substantial change would raise. Our proposals seek to prevent children from being punished for deficiencies in others. School attendance is properly the business of the schools, not the courts. We hope that excluding the courts' jurisdiction will stimulate improvement in our school system, including the development of educational alternatives.

'Exposed to moral danger' is one of the few categories of referral to the juvenile court in which females outnumber males. To understand this, it is important to consider attitudes towards women in our society. Differential socialisation of males and females begins at birth and continues throughout life. As a result of their respective spheres of activity, boys are expected to be adventurous, aggressive, mischievous, creative and independent, whereas girls are expected to be passive, gentle, emotional and dependent. In the juvenile courts and social service agencies this wish to maintain the passive role of women takes the form of 'protection'.

The vast majority of these girls are, however, institutionalised. If the prevention of pregnancy *per se* is the main concern (as it is often said to be), this seems singularly unhelpful. It is very difficult to avoid seeing intervention as punishment for what is considered moral indiscretion. Sex education and availability of contraceptive devices would seem to present more realistic alternatives.

There is little precise information regarding the specific types of cases in the category 'beyond parental control'. It seems generally to include cases where the child has run away or is behaving in a manner which is considered defiant (e.g. staying out late at night). In many of these cases it is clear the child has left home because in some way he or she is having trouble or feels unhappy. Some, for example, may feel the need to be free and want to experience independence; others may be escaping from situations which they find extremely difficult. Referral to court amounts, in effect, to parent–child confrontation: the court and social services are being used to provide formal support to the *parents'* as opposed to the *children's* interests and to maintain their authority within the family unit.

Intervention in each of these circumstances has resulted from particular conceptions of young people and their position in the family and in society. Children and young people are a socially, politically and economically disadvantaged group who, as a result of their powerlessness, are vulnerable to injustice. There is a tendency to keep children dependent, thereby denying them rights and responsibilities. But, as Frank Musgrove writes, 'the young are older than we think'. A healthy society is one which can accept, appreciate and cater for nonconformist behaviour. To force conformity to social expectations is self-defeating and can alienate young people who are doing no more than experiencing the difficulties of growing up. The nature and content of our intervention has failed to recognise their needs and potential.

This does not mean that we should ignore the difficulties children experience. There should be available a wide range of easily accessible services which can provide help and assistance when he or she seeks it: alternative educational programmes, 'crash pads', advice centres and the like.

Emergency intervention would be possible where such children are found to be in circumstances which constitute a substantial and immediate danger to their physical safety. Here the detaining individual (e.g. the police) must inform the child of the reasons for his detention, which may last up to a maximum of 6 hours. Within this time the detaining individual should inform the parents or other responsible person of the reason for detaining the child and should release the child to them as soon as practicable. Where the parents or person responsible cannot be contacted within the time allowed or where the child does not wish to return to his parents, the child would be informed of the existence of the various voluntary services available to him.

Practice

Criteria authorising referral to court should be strictly defined and limited to the following situations:

1. where a child has suffered physical harm or neglect which has been inflicted non-accidentally by his parents*;
2. where a child has been sexually abused by his parents*;
3. where the child has been abandoned by his parents*.

The criteria suggested draw a distinction between situations in which harm or neglect has actually occurred and situations of possible future risk, and also between physical and emotional harm. We have not limited intervention to serious harm or neglect, but, in determining appropriate action, the court would obviously pay particular attention to the nature and circumstances of the parents' act or omission. Repeated minor acts of violence deliberately inflicted justify intervention as much as acts leading to disfigurement or impairment; they may, however, lead to lesser forms of intervention than where serious harm results. The justification for intervention and the nature of that intervention are distinct questions. We have excluded reference to possible abuse or neglect because of the inadequacy of predictive techniques, and to emotional harm because of the subjectivity and unreliability of such judgements. Currently even the most minor injuries can in certain families attract suspicion and precipitate care proceedings. Children labelled 'at risk' attract

* This includes guardian, relative and other members of the household.

particular attention from teaching, nursing, medical and other professional persons who come into contact with them, and it is easy to understand how, in these instances, selective observation can create the impression of abuse or neglect. Concern with conduct based on identifiable and objective criteria is preferable to general feelings of anxiety among professional child-care agencies. Abuse registers would include only those families against whom a court has made a specific finding; the inclusion of children supposedly 'at risk' would be prohibited.

We make one exception to this general principle: the safety of other children in a household where one child has already been abused or neglected. According to Jones and Jones, parents sometimes react to the removal of a child by immediately conceiving another; this clearly causes social services departments further concern and the tendency is to remove such children from their parents at birth. But while aggressive psychopathic parents may assault or neglect more than one child in the family, there is evidence which suggests that individual children can be used as scapegoats – that is, one particular child in the family is the victim of abuse or neglect. Lynch states that, among families who abuse their children and who have more than one child, 80 per cent abuse only one. This means that a balance must be sought between the protection of children from potential harm and the autonomy of the parents. Because social work agencies must be alert to the possibility of harm occurring to the siblings of a battered or neglected child, we acknowledge the need for intervention in such cases. We propose, however, some limits to the nature of such intervention, at least in the first instance. Where one child in the family has been abused or neglected and has, as a result, been removed from the family home, we suggest that other children in the family should be made the subject of supervision orders without further evidence. Such orders should have greater powers than current supervision orders; social workers would have the right to demand entry to the family home and to have access to the children. Emergency removal orders would also be available on any evidence of actual abuse or neglect to an individual child.

We accept that such a narrowing of criteria may entail risks. But the majority of children will benefit by the protection such criteria offer from the potentially harmful consequences of intervention. At the same time, social work agencies will have tangible criteria to guide their actions and may, therefore, be able to adopt a more reflective approach to their responsibilities. Furthermore, the concentration of resources on those who have been harmed may secure for them better services and care than is currently possible.

Emergency removal of a child who seems to meet the criteria specified would be possible on a warrant granted by a family court judge. The applicant would be required to make out a *prima facie* case; this ensures maximum accountability for the decision taken. The applicant would also have to specify his reasons in writing and, where the judge grants the emergency removal order, the judge must also record his reasons in writing for doing so with a note of the evidence which was presented. This order would then be served on the parents (and the child, if appropriate) for the purposes of appeal. Emergency removal orders would be referred back to the court for review within 8 days. The court's decision that the child should remain away from home prior to the adjudication of the referral should be reviewed by the court at 2-weekly intervals in order to take account of any change in the circumstances of the case or of any alternative placement.

The onus would be on the applicant to present evidence (which could be challenged and rebutted by the other parties) and to establish the continued case for the child's removal from home before adjudication. During this period frequent parental contact, unless clearly harmful to the child, must be encouraged. Any decisions to restrict or prevent parental access must be justified in court. Currently a child removed under a place of safety order can be placed far from his parents' home, and this can inhibit parental access. Such placements should be exceptional and justified in court by the applicant. Parental visits should be facilitated by the provision of transport and money where necessary.

At the full hearing of the case there should be a clear distinction between the adjudicatory and dispositional stages, perhaps an interval of 2 to 7 days between the two stages. Proceedings at the adjudicatory stage should be adversarial. The issues for the court to decide are whether or not any harm or neglect has occurred to the child, whether or not the child has been sexually abused, or whether or not the child's family ties have been disrupted. The standard of proof would be that which is currently operative in the civil courts (proof on the balance of probabilities), and the burden of proof would be on the applicant. Matters relating to the child's future would only be considered at the dispositional stage. If the court did not find the alleged criteria proved, the matter would not pr the dispositional stage. Where the case is proved, the child ma court's discretion, be placed in care (preferably foster care) u dispositional stage. The few days between the adjudicatory and the dispositional stage may allow the emotional tensions which can occur when issues of harm, parental fault or neglect are aired in court to subside. This would lead, in the main, to a more rational discussion of the various dispositions available to the court.

The principle of least restrictive alternative

Commentary

Studies of children removed from home and reared in institutions have shown a high level of retardation, mental subnormality and a lack of emotional and physical development. While these conditions are not inevitable, they seem to develop in the absence of consistent stable relationships. Rapid changes of or breakdown in placements and successive periods of institutionalisation are often the hallmark of the career of a child in care. This inability to ensure stability of relationships places such children at a disadvantage and leads us to suggest alternative and less restrictive forms of intervention.

Where the case for compulsory intervention has been made out, the court should intervene in a way which promotes the relationship between the child and his family and which provides the least disruption to the child's life.

Practice

At the disposition hearing the burden would be on the applicant to *show the need for compulsory intervention.* The fact that one or more of the specific criteria have been proved would not automatically lead to intervention. The court must be satisfied that the intervention proposed would be beneficial to the child. The court could at this stage, therefore, either make no order or choose from among several disposition alternatives. The agency seeking to remove the child or otherwise intervene with the family must present to the court some planned programme, and the child and his family (perhaps through their lawyer) would be able to offer alternative responses. The court must also be satisfied that the proposed disposition facilities are, in fact, available for the particular child.

Currently dispositions in care proceedings are primarily a choice between care orders, which vest parental rights in a local authority, and supervision orders, which enable the local authority to supervise the child at home. Although there is a consensus among child-care experts on the child's need for a continuous and stable environment, children who are removed from home are sometimes denied this. Constant parental figures, belonging to a particular cultural or ethnic identity, are important aspects of the child's home environment. We suggest that there should be a far wider range of dispositions to enable the child to remain at home whenever possible. These could include domestic services in the home, social education of the parents, medical treatment and day-care provision for the child.

These dispositions are designed to alleviate and correct the particular harm suffered by the child. Intervention should be directed at the immediate and particular difficulty presented; the provision of additional services which might improve the child's and family's general environment can only be offered on a voluntary basis. It must be remembered that not all acts of abuse and neglect are committed by sadistic or aggressive parents; they may be caused by sudden loss of control through the stress of modern life (exacerbated by isolation resulting from the break-up of communities and of the extended family, inadequate housing, financial difficulties and immaturity). While arguments for social and economic reform are beyond the scope of this book, the provision of family services and support would alleviate some of the factors which can lead to child abuse and child neglect. Kempe and Kempe point out that abusive parents tend to be isolated, without friends or confidants, and have trouble turning to others for help. Crisis centres and emergency telephone numbers would provide a lifeline for such families; at the same time, domestic help and parental education may remove some of the pressures from parents and perform a rehabilitative function. Day nurseries not only help the parent who is unable to cope during the day, but provide support and educational groups for parents suffering depression and isolation.

The applicant seeking removal of the child from his family should, in addition to proving the need for removal, state the reasons why alternative (and less restrictive) dispositions are unsatisfactory. This reflects the principle of parental autonomy and encourages social workers to consider the possibilities of working *with* families rather than *against* them.

Where it is necessary to remove the child from home, the court would have responsibility for the specific arrangements and would not delegate this to local-authority social service departments. The court would specify the nature of the placement: with relatives, in a foster home, in a residential home or whatever. Currently a care order is granted on the assumption that a particular placement will be available; this ideal may never materialise. The result is that a child may remain some months in a temporary placement and may then be moved to the second- or third-choice placement. Judicial overview of the child's placement may prevent this. Reasons for the choice of disposition must be given in writing and form the grounds for an appeal. Failure to implement the plan would also be a ground of appeal.

Every effort should be made to re-establish the child who has been removed from home with his family. Parents should be encouraged to participate in their child's care by attending such activities as meetings and reviews, buying clothes and taking the child to keep medical appointments. Frequent parental access would continue unless denied or restricted by the court. Where the child is removed from home, the placement would be reviewed in court at 6-monthly intervals for 18 months after the child's removal and, thereafter, at the court's discretion. The applicants at the review proceedings would have to state why the order should continue, provide evidence of the child's progress over the previous 6 months and propose a programme for the next period. The child and his parents would be able to challenge each element of these proceedings. In renewing the order the court would be governed by the same principles which affected the original decision. By this continuous monitoring of parental and local-authority performance the court would be able to ensure that the objectives of intervention are achieved and prevent children remaining away from home by default.

During this period parental rights are not revoked but are suspended and remain with the court (as in wardship currently). Where there has been no contact between the parents and the child for 18 months, however, the court *may* revoke parental rights and vest them in the local authority. This would be possible only where the local authority presents to the court plans (acceptable to the court and to a specially appointed 'guardian *ad litem*') for the long-term non-residential placement of the child. Even where parental rights have been vested in the local authority, the child, parents, local authority or any person on behalf of the child would be able to refer to the court any-matter in respect of the child (except where the child has been adopted). This provides some protection to the child from the bureaucracy to which his care has been entrusted and includes the right to apply at any time for a revocation of the local authority's parental rights.

Where a supervision or other service order has been made by the court, this would lapse automatically after 18 months. It would not be possible for supervision orders to become care orders. Where it is sought to remove a supervised child from his home, there must be fresh proceedings based on some new evidence of harm or neglect to the child.

The principle of the parties' right to legal representation

Commentary

The case for separate legal representation for all parties is fully discussed in Chapter 7.

Practice

Court procedures must be fair, and protect the legal rights of all concerned. The child should at every stage of the proceedings be a full and independent party with an advocate assigned to act on his behalf. He would be automatically given legal aid. Parents would also be full and independent parties with entitlement to legal representation and, if necessary, legal aid.

Independent lawyers for all the parties would ensure that procedural rights were maintained and would guard against inaccurate presentation of facts. Lawyers would be able to interpret the court proceedings to the parties and ensure that their views are heard.

In order to ensure that the parties have proper notice of all the issues, evidence would be on affidavits, which would be exchanged in advance of the hearing. Full disclosure of evidence would facilitate the role of the child's and parents' advocates and enable all parties to foresee and meet the issues in dispute. Discovery of documents, including medical records, reports and files of social services, would be available to all legal representatives. Such documents may hold a considerable amount of information about a family, accumulated over a period of years. Parties must have the right of access to this and, where appropriate, to question it. This ensures greater fairness and efficiency in the conduct of proceedings than currently.

Since individual rights and personal liberties are at stake, proceedings should be adversarial in nature to ensure full testing of all the issues in the case. The court should not adopt the role of inquisitor and enter into the conflicts between the parties, but should assess the evidence presented to it. There may, however, be difficulties (caused by the youth and immaturity of the child) in the role of the child's advocate. He should adopt an investigatory approach to the proceedings, by calling, for example, for independent social work or other reports; these would be paid for within the legal aid scheme. This means that lawyers would have to have a broad working knowledge of the various services available for families in difficulties. Wherever the child is old enough to express a view, that view should not be usurped by professionals allegedly acting in his best interests. Appointing a lawyer to represent the child and his views will prevent the conflicts which currently arise in care proceedings where the child, advocate and 'guardian *ad litem*' may all disagree, or where the child's lawyer feels he should represent the views of the parents.

The principle of visibility and accountability of decision-making

Commentary

We have already discussed the subjective nature of the existing civil jurisdiction of courts dealing with children. Our aim is to limit the discretionary powers which this has created and to recommend firm guidelines for decisions at each stage of the proceeding.

Practice

Formal criteria for referral to the court have been set out. Reasons for all decisions would have to be given in writing – for example, why the grounds for intervention are made out and why a particular disposition was chosen. All decisions of the courts would be subject to appellate review.

There should also be a children's Ombudsman, in each regional area, to watch over the care of children who have been removed from home. The Ombudsman would be able to review decisions made by local-authority agencies and to hear grievances from children and families. He would have power to refer to the court any matters referred to him by the child or persons concerned about the child.

Conclusion – a time for action

For nearly a decade family courts have received support in principle from lawyers, social workers and politicians: for example, the Labour Party Manifesto of 1974 and reports from 'Justice' in 1975, from the Conservative Party Lawyers Group in 1978 and from the Law Society in 1979. But little has been achieved in practice. A year after the 1974 election commitment to introduce family courts, the Secretary of State for Social Services, Barbara Castle, stated in Parliament that 'there was no prospect of the Government accepting the recommendations for family courts', and there had not been (by mid-1979) as much as a Green Paper on the cost of implementation. Cost is the most frequently expressed reason for non-implementation, but family courts would not necessarily be costly. Indeed, implementation of our proposals would cost *less* than the present structure. Limited criteria for intervention mean that the judicial system and the professions which seek to deal with children in trouble would be able to concentrate their efforts and resources on a more narrowly defined group of children. While the debate continues, the future of thousands of families is being determined by a network of courts which has been described as 'chaotic' and 'patchwork', and which cannot provide justice for children.

Bibliography

Allen, F. (1964) *The Borderland of Criminal Justice* (University of Chicago Press).

Andenaes, J. (1966) 'The General Preventive Effects of Punishment', *University of Pennsylvania Law Review*, vol. cxiv, no. 7, p. 969.

Anderson, R. (1978) *Representation in the Juvenile Court* (London: Routledge).

Belson, W. (1975) *Juvenile Theft: the Causal Factors* (London: Harper and Row).

Berlins, M. and Wansell, G. (1974) *Caught in the Act* (Harmondsworth: Penguin).

Booth, M. and Harris, B. (eds) (1977) Hall, Sir W. Clarke and Morrison, A. C. L., *The Law Relating to Children and Young Persons* (London: Butterworth).

Bowlby, J. (1946) *Forty-four Juvenile Thieves* (London: Bailliere, Tindall and Cox).

British Assocation of Social Workers (1975) Evidence to House of Commons Expenditure Committee in *Eleventh Report, Children and Young Persons Act 1969*, vol. ii, HC 5341–1ii (London: HMSO).

British Association of Social Workers (1977) *Social workers and a policy in relation to the Children and Young Persons' Act 1969* (Birmingham: BASW).

British Association of Social Workers (1978) *The Central Child Abuse Register* (Birmingham: BASW).

Brody, S. R. (1976) *The Effectiveness of Sentencing*, HORU Study No. 35 (London: HMSO).

Bruce, N. and Spencer, J. (1976) *Face to Face with Families* (Edinburgh: Macdonald).

Buckle, J. (1978) 'Police Involvement in N.A.I.', *Social Work Today*, no. 9, p. 25.

Carpenter, M. (1852) *Evidence to Select Committee on Criminal and Destitute Juveniles* (London: HMSO).

Cawson, P. *et al.* (1978) *Young Offenders in Care*, preliminary report (unpublished).

Cicourel, A. (1976) *The Social Organisation of Juvenile Justice* (London: Heinemann).

Committee of Inquiry into the Care and Supervision Provided in Relation to Maria Colwell (1974) *Report* (London: HMSO).

Committee on Children and Young Persons (1960) *The Ingleby Report*, Cmnd. 1191 (London: HMSO).

Committee on Children and Young Persons, Scotland (1964) *The Kilbrandon Report*, Cmnd. 2306 (Edinburgh: HMSO).

Committee on Local Authority and Allied Personal Social Services (1968) *The Seebohm Report*, Cmnd. 3703 (London: HMSO).

Committee on One Parent Families (1974) *The Finer Report*, Cmnd. 5629 (London: HMSO).

Conservative Political Centre (1978) *The Case for Family Courts* (London: CPC).

Cressey, D., and McDermot, R. (1973) *Diversion from the Juvenile Justice System* (University of Michigan).

Davies, M. (1974) 'Social Inquiry for the Courts', *British Journal of Criminology*, vol. 14, no. 1, pp. 18–33.

Department of Health and Social Security (1973) *Further survey by social work services division* (unpublished).

Department of Health and Social Security (1975) *Non-Accidental Injury to Children* (London: HMSO).

Department of Health and Social Security (1976) *Observations on the Report from the Select Committee on Violence in Marriage*, Cmnd. 6690 (London: HMSO).

Department of Health and Social Security (1978) *Violence to Children*, Cmnd. 7123 (London: HMSO).

Didrichsen, J. (1979) 'In Practice', *Community Care*, 22 February.

Ditchfield, J. (1976) *Police Cautioning in England and Wales*, HORU Study No. 37 (London: HMSO).

Duxbury, E. (1973) *Evaluation of Youth Service Bureaus* (Sacramento: Californian Youth Authority).

Farrington, D. (1977) 'The effects of public labelling', *British Journal of Criminology*, vol. 17, no. 2, pp. 112–25.

Feldman, L. (1978) *Care Proceedings* (London: Oyez).

Fitzherbert, K. (1976) 'The Power of the Social Worker over Children in Long-Term Care', paper presented at the Voice of the Child in Care Conference – quoted in Nicholas, C., 'Who Cares?', unpublished MA dissertation (Brunel University, 1976) p. 3.

Foster, B. *et al.* (1977) *Child Care – a cause for concern* (Birmingham: Movement of Practising Psychologists).

Freeman, M. D. A. (1976) 'Children in Care: the Impact of the Children Act 1975', *Family Law*, vol. 6, no. 3, pp. 136–41.

Freeman, M. D. A. (1979) 'Retaining a Child in Care', *New Law Journal*, vol. 129, no. 5893, pp. 223–4.

Giller, H. and Morris, A. (1979) 'Supervision Orders: the Routinization of Treatment', *Howard Journal*, pp. 149–59.

Goldstein, J. *et al.* (1973) *Beyond the Best Interests of the Child* (New York: Free Press).

Hall, J. G. (1970) *Proposal for a Family Court* (London: National Council for One Parent Families).

Hall, J. G. (1978) *A Unified Family Court* (London: National Council for One Parent Families).

Harris, B. (1978) 'The Juvenile Court: Time to give way to the Family Court, *Family Law*, vol. 8, no. 2, pp. 68–73.

Hayes, M. (1978) 'Separate Representation of Children in Care Proceedings', *Family Law*, vol. 8, pp. 91–6.

Hill, M. D. (1855) *Practical Suggestions to the Founders of Reformatory Schools* (London: Cash).

Holman, R. (1975) 'The Place of Fostering in Social Work', *British Journal of Social Work*, vol. 5, no. 1, pp. 3–27.

Holman, R. (1976) *Inequality in Child Care* (London: Child Poverty Action Group).

Home Office (1948) Circular No. 160/1948, 8 July 1948.

Home Office (1965) *The Child, the Family and the Young Offender*, Cmnd. 2742 (London: HMSO).

Home Office (1968) *Children in Trouble*, Cmnd. 3601 (London: HMSO).

Home Office (1970) *Care and treatment in a planned environment* (London: HMSO).

Home Office (1976) Circular No. 176/76, 18 November 1976.

Home Office, Welsh Office, Department of Health and Social Security, Department of Education and Science (1976) *Observations on the Eleventh Report from the Expenditure Committee*, Cmnd. 6491 (London: HMSO).

House of Commons Expenditure Committee (1975) *Eleventh Report, Children and Young Persons Act 1969*, vols I and II, HC 534–ii (London: HMSO).

Institute of Judicial Administration and American Bar Association (1977) *Juvenile Justice Standards Project*, vols 1–24, *Standards for Juvenile Justice: a summary and analysis* (Cambridge, Mass.: Ballinger).

Jackson, J. *et al.* (eds) (1979) *Rayden on Divorce*, vols 1 and 2 (London: Butterworth).

Jones, R. and Jones, C. (1978) 'A Social Perspective' in Lee, C. M. (ed.), *Child Abuse: Reader and Source Book* (Milton Keynes: Open University Press).

Justice (1976) *Report on Parental Rights and Duties in Custody Suits* (London: Justice).

Kellmer Pringle, M. (1975) *The Needs of Children* (London: Hutchinson).

Kempe, C. and Helfer, R. (eds) (1976) *Child Abuse and Neglect* (Cambridge, Mass.: Ballinger).

Kempe, R. S. and Kempe, C. (1978) *Child Abuse* (London: Fontana/Open Books).

Labour Party Study Group (1964) *Crime – a challenge to us all* (London: Transport House).

Lambeth, Southwark and Lewisham Area Health Authority, Inner London Probation and After-care Committee (1975) *Report of the Joint Committee of Inquiry into Non-Accidental Injury to Children with particular reference to the case of Lisa Godfrey* (unpublished).

Law Society (1979) *A Better Way Out* (London: Law Society).

Levin, J. (1975) 'The Legal Representation of Children', *Family Law*, vol. 5, no. 3, pp. 129–34.

Lipton, D. *et al.* (1975) *The Effectiveness of Correctional Treatment* (New York: Praeger).

Lynch, M. (1978) 'The Critical Path' in Lee, C. M. (ed.), *Child Abuse: Reader and Source Book* (Milton Keynes: Open University Press).

McCabe, S. *et al.* (1978) *Defining Crime* (Oxford: Blackwell).

Magistrates' Association (1975) Evidence to House of Commons Expenditure Committee in *Eleventh Report, Children and Young Persons Act 1969*, vol. II, HC 5341–1ii (London: HMSO).

Magistrates' Association, the Association of Metropolitan Authorities and the Association of County Councils (1978) *Report of Joint Working Party, Children and Young Persons Act 1969* (London: Association of County Councils).

Martin, H. P. (1976) *The Abused Child* (Cambridge, Mass.: Ballinger).

Millham, S. *et al.* (1978) *Locking up Children* (Farnborough: Saxon House).

MIND Report 14 (1975) *The Act on Trial* (London: MIND).

Morris, A. (1978) 'Diversion of Juvenile Offenders from the Criminal Justice System' in Tutt, N. (ed.), *Alternative Strategies for Coping with Crime* (London: Martin Roberston).

Morris, A. (1978) *Juvenile Justice?* (London: Heinemann).

Morris, A. and Giller, H. (1977) 'The Juvenile Court – the Client's Perspective', *Criminal Law Review*, pp. 198–205.

Morris, A. and Giller, H. (1978) 'Lawyers and the Juvenile Court', *LAG Bulletin*, October.

Morris, A. and Giller, H. (1979) 'Juvenile Justice and Social Work in Britain' in Parker, H. (ed.), *Social Work and the Courts* (London: Edward Arnold).

Morris, P. (1978) 'Police: By Invitation Only?', *Community Care*, 22 March.

Musgrove, F. (1968) 'Why Youths Riot: The Adolescent Ghetto' in Heman,

M., Sadofsky, S. and Rosenberg, B. (eds) *Work, Youth and Unemployment* (New York: Thomas Y. Crowell).

National Children's Review (1972) *From Birth to Seven* (London: Longman).

Newman, N. *et al.* (1975) *A roof over their heads: residential provision in South East Scotland* (University of Edinburgh Department of Social Administration).

Nottinghamshire Social Services Department (1975) *Report of the Project Concerning Children in Care and Related Issues* (Nottinghamshire Social Services Department).

Page, R. and Clark, G. (1977) *Who Cares?* (London: National Children's Bureau).

Parsloe, P. (1978) *Juvenile Justice in Britain and the United States* (London: Routledge).

Pease, K. (1978) 'Community Service and the Tariff', *Criminal Law Review*, p. 269.

Pinchbeck, I. and Hewitt, M. (1969) *Children in English Society*, vol. 1, *From Tudor Times to the Eighteenth Century* (London: Routledge).

Pinchbeck, I. and Hewitt, M. (1973) *Children in English Society*, vol. 2, *From the Eighteenth Century to the Children Act, 1948* (London: Routledge).

Police Federation (1975) Evidence to House of Commons Expenditure Committee in *Eleventh Report, Children and Young Persons Act 1969*, vol. II, HC 5341–1ii (London: HMSO).

Poor Law Commission (1842) *Report on an Inquiry into the Sanitary Conditions of the Labouring Population of Great Britain* (London: HMSO).

Power, M. *et al.* (1974) 'Delinquency and the Family', *British Journal of Social Work*, vol. 4, no. 1, pp. 13–38.

President's Commission on Law Enforcement and Administration of Justice (1967) *Task Force Report: Juvenile Deliquency and Youth Crime* (Washington: US Government Printing Office).

Priestley, P. *et al.* (1977) *Justice for Juveniles* (London: Routledge).

Pringle, M. K. (1975) *The Needs of Children* (London: Hutchinson).

Reynolds, D. (1976) 'When Pupils and Teachers Refuse a Truce' in Mungham, G. and Pearson, G. (eds), *Working Class Youth Cultures* (London: Routledge).

Rutter, M. *et al.* (1979) *Fifteen Thousand Hours* (London: Open Books).

Samuels, A. (1976) 'The Children Act 1975', *Family Law*, vol. 6, no. 1, pp. 5–8.

Sarri, R. and Hasenfeld, Y. (eds) (1976) *Brought to Justice* (Ann Arbor: National Assessment of Juvenile Corrections, University of Michigan).

Schneider, M. *et al.* (1976) 'A Predictive Screening Questionnaire for Potential Problems in Mother Child Interaction' in Kempe, C. and Helfer, F. (eds), *Child Abuse and Neglect* (Cambridge, Mass.: Ballinger).

Schwartz, R. D. *et al.* (1967) 'On Legal Sanctions', *University of Chicago Law Review*, vol. xxxiv, p. 274.

Select Committee on Violence in the Family (1977) *Violence to Children*, vols 1–3 (London: HMSO).

Shearer, A. (1978) 'Tragedies Revisited', *Social Work Today*, no. 10, pp. 19–21.

Somerset Area Review Committee for Non-accidental Injury to Children (1977) *Wayne Brewer: Report of the review panel* (Taunton: County Hall).

Sparks, R. F. *et al.* (1977) *Surveying victims* (Chichester: Wiley).

Thorpe, R. (1974) 'Mum and Mrs. So and So', *Social Work Today*, vol. 4, no. 22, pp. 691–5.

Titmuss, R. (1953) 'The Family as a Social Institution' in *Report of the British National Conference on Social Work* (London: National Institute of Social Work).

Tutt, N. (1976) 'Recomittals of Juvenile Offenders' in *British Journal of Criminology*, vol. 16, no. 4, pp. 385–8.

Walter, J. (1978) *Sent Away* (Farnborough: Saxon House).

Walton, R. (1976) 'The Best Interests of the Child', *British Journal of Social Work*, vol. 6, no. 4, pp. 307–13.

Welsh, M. (1975) 'State Intervention on Behalf of Neglected Children – Search for Realistic Standards, *Stamford Law Review*, no. 27, p. 985.

White, S. (1973) 'Federal Programmes for Young Children: Review and Recommendations', referred to in Institute of Judicial Administration and American Bar Association, *Juvenile Justice Standards Project: Standards Relating to Abuse and Neglect* (Cambridge, Mass.: Ballinger, 1977).

Willcock, H. and Stokes, J. (1968) *Deterrents to Crime among Youths aged 15 to 21* (London: Government Social Survey).

Williams, J. (1978) 'Child Abuse, Child Care, and the Law-Failures of State Intervention', *Family Law*, vol. 8, no. 4, pp. 228–37.

Wilson, H. and Herbert, G. (1978) *Parents and Children in the Inner City* (London: Routledge).

Wolfgang, M. (1976) 'Seriousness of crime and a policy of juvenile justice' in Short, J. (ed.), *Delinquency, Crime and Society* (University of Chicago Press).

Wolfgang, M. *et al.* (1972) *Delinquency in a birth cohort* (University of Chicago Press).

Yule, W. and Raynes, R. D. (1972) 'The Behavioural Characteristics of Children in Residential Care in Relation to Indices of Separation', *Journal of Child Psychology and Psychiatry*, no. 13, pp. 249–58.

Zander, M. (1975) 'What Happens to Young Offenders in Care', *New Society*, 24 July.